Penguin Education

Penguin Education Specials
General Editor: Willem van der Eyken

Education for a Change
Community Action and the School
Colin and Mog Ball

Colin Ball's education was interrupted by the usual ration of school and four years at the University of Keele, studying geography and geology. Surviving this, he worked as a teacher in Birmingham, Malaya, and Ghana, and since 1970 has directed the Advisory Service for Schools at Community Service Volunteers.

Mog Ball was also handicapped by school and university, becoming a teacher in Stoke-on-Trent and Ghana, and now getting into education, at last, by looking after their two children.

Education for a Change
Community Action and the School
Colin and Mog Ball

Illustrations by Jeremy Long

Penguin Education

Penguin Education
A Division of Penguin Books Ltd,
Harmondsworth, Middlesex, England
Penguin Books Inc, 7110 Ambassador Road,
Baltimore, Md 21207, USA
Penguin Books Australia Ltd
Ringwood, Victoria, Australia

First published 1973

Made and printed in Great Britain by
C. Nicholls & Company Ltd
Set in Monotype Plantin

Contents

Preface

Community Service is an acceptable idea to most people. Whatever your reservations about ways and means, it isn't very easy to come out hard and fast against the idea of people helping one another. So it's quite a good platform to mount, community service. The applause is guaranteed.

Working on the subject of incorporating community service into education programmes, we became aware that what education needed wasn't community service, but a good shake-up. Too often injections of 'good things' contributed to the survival of bad things. And gained a bad name in the process. But 'helping one another' was so radically different from the 'survival of the fittest' philosophy which pervades the schools we saw, that we felt it necessary to offer a more fundamental contribution to education. This book is not about injections for survival, it is about administering a fatal dose.

Visits to schools, visits from kids, listening to ordinary people – that constituted the research for this book. It was from the most ordinary of mums, dads, schoolkids and bar leaners that we learnt how widespread is the feeling that school is out. And when we tried out a few of the suggestions made in this book on these people they didn't say, 'That's a good idea', but rather 'That's what I've always thought!' So, in the hope that this will ring a bell for more ordinary school kids, and ordinary people in general, we would like to thank the ones who talked and listened: Kofi Adjei, Joe and Pat Hall, Ernie Bowles, Harry Van Praag, Alec Dickson, Doug and Nell Revell, Keith Tomkinson, Tanya Chapman and her friend Maggie Allchorne, 'Iron' Owarre, Cliff Edwards, Allan Leadbeater, George Ojo, Nick Blake, Brian and Sandy Ritchie, Ron and Bea Gross, Willem and Jeanette Bakker, Chris and Bobby Bailey, Minnie Williams and her mother Daisy, Jack Durham, Harford Thomas, Nick Ashwell, Patrick Ankrah, and Andrew and Diana Quarmby.

Especially we should like to thank Mary Reding, who was always enthusiastic when we were depressed, and typed the manuscript for us; Charles Beresford of the Homerton Teachers' Centre, Cambridge, for his help with Chapter 9; our parents, who helped so much by looking after our children while we wrote this book, and Jonathan Croall, our editor, who helped so much by looking after us.

The cartoon strips which precede chapters 2, 4 and 5 were drawn by Jeremy Long for CSV's School and Community Kits. They were intended to help kids who couldn't read very well. Fill in the bubbles yourself!

Introduction

There is a possibility that somebody has already written this book. But, the jargon of educationists being what it is, we didn't understand it when we read it. It seems particularly sad that a book about education should be difficult to read, since everybody is at some stage in the process of being educated and therefore has a vested interest in educational theory; at least, in those theories which suggest that education is more than the book-learning you get in school, that its aims are further-reaching than the O-levels for which some sweat blood. So to begin with it seemed worthwhile to write a book which would be understood by the young people in our educational institutions, as well as those below them in the educational hierarchy: teachers, headmasters, Chief Education Officers, researchers, the Schools Council. Later it became clear that the way we educate is a subject of universal relevance, so that it seemed even more important to shout loudly the irrelevance of what we call education in Great Britain today.

Generally we will be discussing the role of young people as consumers in the education industry, because youth is the time when most education is considered most necessary. Eventually we hope to show that our ideas are not confined to those under twenty-one. But for the moment let us think of the school-kid as consumer. The outlets for his voice are burgeoning: *Children's Rights*, (now called *Kids*) *Schoolkids Oz*, and schools action unions. Our primary schools are admired abroad for their child-centred developments and their experiments in cooperative learning (made despite the impending encounter with the eleven plus). At home, however, the high master of a public school advocates a counter-revolution against the progressive teaching methods of primary schools: 'It may be progressive for all the children in the class to build the Eiffel Tower together with Shredded Wheat boxes', he says, 'but the inevitable result is disorder and illiteracy.'[1] And, there you are, our secondary schools are filled with disorderly illiterates. Of course, being the high master of a secondary school, he sadly did not question secondary teaching methods. It seems that the consumers must do this. They must not acquiesce in the role of the consumer who takes the good advice of his magazine and buys the best: the school with the best rugger team, best A-level results and Oxbridge entrance. They must be the feet-first, I-want-my-rights consumers, the investigators of the inadequacies of the system in which they are enmeshed, the callers for an education that will have some meaning in the life they are to lead. In Africa a student will stand up smartly in class immediately the teacher digresses from the syllabus and insist that he returns to relevant topics at once. The syllabus may be a mistake but the student's attitude is unquestionable – he is the consumer and he knows what he wants to learn.

There is an ambivalence in our view of young people. We admire them if they take initiative, do exciting things, show prowess, courage and intelligence. But they should know their place, and one place is that they have no right to question the form of the educational process they go through, or its content. True, many schools now have a 'school council'. On visits to secondary schools in our work we usually ask if there is such a council. Since our audience has been assembled in the hall for a double period's talk on community service, they sometimes muster surprise at the question and look anxiously at 'sir' when asked what the council does. 'Smoking rooms and long hair, is it?' we ask. 'Well, next time it meets, try standing up and saying something like this – Sirs, it would seem to us that the world is in a terrible mess – war, poverty, loneliness, starvation, disease, crime, uncontrolled technology and all the rest of it. Is what we are learning in this school really preparing us to *cope* with these things, let alone to try to *change* them?'

Talk of 'pupil power' and 'pupils' rights' sounds rather flashy and sensation-seeking in a book about community service as an educational resource. Our work has taken us into many schools both directly and indirectly. We are directly invited to give talks to pupils about community service. Indirectly we published kits of advice for teachers and social workers and we met many of them at day conferences and workshops. On the whole we found that pupils were dramatically more responsive to our ideas, and more enthusiastic about them, than were the bulk of the staff. Kids came into the classroom expecting to hear how they must go out of their school to help the sick, the aged and the handicapped, to fight pollution and to serve the community. There was always some surprise when they found us, for at least part of our address, encouraging them to stand up for themselves, because only then could they stand up for others and avoid being 'others' themselves one day. 'Activity' is what we advocate, because we believe our schools are encouraging 'passivity', a 'passivity' which has become an all-pervading element in our society. We are advocating not 'help your neighbour', but something which somebody else has already labelled 'conviviality'. We do not say that it is 'good for you' to be active and convivial with others, but that it seems a logical and effective way of being a human being as opposed to a passive, harassed, dominated or dominating blob.

Perhaps we don't speak in quite that polemical tone. Instead we say the same things by telling of the work that some young people are already doing in the community; we describe ideas we have for widening the scope of that work and talk of 'people-oriented' education. These subjects are straightforward enough and this book will be concerned with them. The implications go deep.

One of these implications we mistakenly let slip when speaking to an adult group, a mixture of social workers, youth workers, policemen, teachers and educational administrators. 'Young people represent the most potent force for change in our society,' we said. Whether it was true or not, it certainly wasn't acceptable to that audience. Yet in it lies the very foundation of our thought on community service and the interaction between school and community. We believe that, if this potent force is educated in a way that enables it to effect changes, this ability to effect change will become its skill. The society that these people make will be their own and not their manipulator.

It is difficult, because of the unacceptability of this basic premise for many teachers, to speak to them in the same way that we speak to their pupils. With them, this is our usual line of argument: in the past we have been encouraging young people to perform service to the community. Is this right? Why should they paper over other peoples' cracks? Undoubtedly the more intelligent soon decide that they are plugging gaps in an inadequate social system and become disenchanted and cynical. On the other hand, the less intelligent have no idea why they are doing it, let alone why the problems exist. We would like to suggest a new approach, an approach based on the *right* of a young person to participate in a way that he can understand and appreciate, which will involve changes in education itself.

Then follow the same stories that the pupils hear. The teachers listen and are interested, but only rarely do they take up the ideas with the verve of the younger audience. Which is why we hope that some pupils will read what we have to say, as well as their teachers.

Schools have different kinds of relationships with their local community. Some see no point in any kind of links. Others, more sensibly, see the school as a focal point of community life. Surprisingly few see the school as providing any kind of service *for* the local community. Most schools consider themselves part of a nationwide educational system, doing much the same as any other school, though proud, here and there, of their 'unique' experiments. This isolation of school from community can best be demonstrated by asking pupils what they want to do when they leave school. The standard answers are there – university, teacher, nurse, scientist. Many can make no reply – the young people who can make no choice. These are the ones who drift into the local supermarkets, the local building sites, the local factories. But in no case, whether the pupil is destined to 'win' or 'lose', to break the links with the local community or to be tied to it, is the answer made in terms of what can be done in the local community. Few school children have any real knowledge about their local community or, more particularly, about their own importance in it. The true community school should not just provide an education for the whole community, it must provide a whole range of services for the community, services based on truly relevant and practical education.

Some teachers have come to recognize service to the community in its crudest form as a way of showing young people that the place they live in has its own distinctive problems, for which local people have responsibility. This is where the trouble begins.

A teacher, let us call him Mr Smith, is in charge of community service in a school. Naturally he wants to begin by discovering where his pupils can 'help'. He soon learns that this is difficult. He might try the local psychiatric or subnormality hospital, having read in the papers, perhaps, about the glaring deficiencies of such institutions. He may even find that the hospital boasts a Voluntary Help Organizer. But he is advised – not by the Voluntary Help Organizer necessarily, more probably by his own colleagues and parents – that 'children shouldn't be exposed to this kind of experience'. Well, he thinks, he'll give that one a miss and turns to the local general hospital. Here it is a definite mistake to go and offer help. 'What makes you think we need help?' is the message exuded by a guided tour of spotless wards and smiling patients, even in geriatric and long-stay wards. Baffled and confused he reads the Seebohm Report and his eyes bulge when he sees that social services departments are advised to make the fullest possible use of volunteers. But at the social services department he finds that 'no volunteer liaison officer has yet been appointed' though he leaves with a good long list of all the old people's homes and children's homes in the area. He leaves too, with the knowledge that: 'Casework and problem families can't be dealt with by kids, old boy.' Undaunted, he tries the homes: 'Work of this kind needs professionals, not amateurs.' 'Well, we could have a couple of kids in to chat to a few of them ....' 'What can your children do that our staff can't, Mr Smith?' 'And what will happen when all the children go off on holiday?' And so, in the end, Mr Smith's school visit some old people, give out Christmas parcels and raise money for Shelter by sponsored walks.

How appalling. Because like so many other things we do in school, this 'subject' cannot be appealing or interesting to everyone in the class. Some may be enthralled by a long conversation with an eighty year old about the Boer War; others are bored and embarrassed.

This is not cause for total depression, though. There are many examples of professionals taking the plunge and allowing young people into their establishments. There are many who seek actively to encourage this invasion and it is often thanks to them that what we later descibe has occurred. But progress is limited by those avenues which cannot be explored and developed – unless we change the approach.

There are various possibilities. The ultimate is a complete deprofessionalization of function, so that all who are willing to participate are allowed to do so, with no hindrance either from the individual professional or the union. If one stipulates 'a right to participate' or 'a right to be active in community life' we must envisage a situation where it becomes wrong to discriminate against the non-professional. Training would thus become less important than willingness. The learning would take place 'on the job', as it already does in certain spheres, and education would be concerned with encouraging willingness and activity. Such apprentice-style learning would be complemented by a community-oriented curriculum.

But in the near future, and perhaps more realistically, the young people can take matters into their own hands. We have indicated a starting point: a more realistically oriented curriculum in the school. The next stage is for them to consider on whose terms they are going to serve the community. Are they to serve the community under the present terms, of imposition on the part of the teacher, of condescension on the part of the professional? Or are they to make the choice themselves, not only of what they are to do, but how they are to do it?

We once met an art teacher who told us of an experience which he had had with an art class. The story lacks one ingredient for a perfect piece of community involvement, but it illustrates in many ways the change of approach we are proposing.

This teacher had been having some trouble with one of his classes, the notorious fourth-year leavers. To most of them, the art class had no meaning, but it offered ample scope for what one might call 'light relief'. The teacher was under a heavy barrage, not only from the class, but from cleaners who had to clear up the mess, from teachers of neighbouring classes who complained about the noise, and from parents who complained to the headmaster of painted shoes and tie-dyed shirts. The teacher tackled this apparently insoluble problem by visiting the matron of a local hospital, not to seek advice about his developing medical condition, but to ask *her* help.

The art class gave no more trouble. Every week easels and boards were set up in one of the hospital wards. They brought something no professional could provide: a break, a change in routine, a hustle and bustle; and the patients could enjoy what we all enjoy – a chance to watch other people work. To the class, art became something real, something to be shared. And what better place to paint a bowl of fruit?

The missing ingredient was the fact that the class was an imposition. But if those young people had themselves realized or engineered such an option, we do not think any of them would have refused it. The reluctance to accept help by the professionals did not occur because the art master himself was asking for help. Moreover, he did not offer 'thirty young volunteers' but a package deal, an art class.

On whose terms did it all happen? On the terms of the young people: they were doing what they enjoyed. They did it for the community and the local people and they offered something that a professional could not give. They also were learning a little about their local community and the fact that they could be active in it and that they could be important at something. The hospital became a resource for learning, the school was providing a service for the hospital.

We have talked about the frustrations facing the teacher and the protective attitude of the professional. The approach which we have exemplified in the story of the art class can overcome both, but how can we encourage it to occur more widely? Let us suppose for a moment that our Mr Smith was rather more successful than earlier described. He has a number of projects lined up for his pupils and he decides to initiate them with lessons on social problems as they exist in the local community. But, sadly, he finds that his talk about the plight of the elderly, or the institutionalization of the mentally handicapped, doesn't exactly leave the class speechless with rage and bursting to do something. It all means nothing to them.

Then, to make matters worse, the pupils find themselves not grappling with some urgent social problems, but doing rather meaningless and peripheral jobs – handing out tea or scrubbing down walls. In the end the experience is forgotten because it wasn't understood, or regarded cynically as how 'they' wouldn't let 'us' help. If those same young people were being asked not 'to do' this or to 'help' them, but simply allowed and encouraged to do things their way, to do things they enjoyed, were skilled at, understood, as in the case of the art class and some of the examples described later, then everybody – young person, professional, teacher, school and community – would have benefited. 'Don't give me this service lark, give me a job to do.'

We will try to show how we feel this can be done.

1 The Short Happy Life of the Young Volunteer

Is it naïvely optimistic to say that we have, off and on, been helping one another since time immemorial? However, now it's said, that's it. If you ask a child for an example from history of this simple kind of service, you will probably be told about the good Samaritan. Whether that story is true or not is beside the point. It indicates something about our thoughts and beliefs, and it seems to have rung a bell for a few hundred years. Presumably all those other peoples one flips through quickly in history lessons – the Assyrians, the Hittites, Babylonians and even the ravaging Vikings and Vandals – had within them this brotherly spirit. But we have no intention here of chronicling the fluctuations of the helping relationship, historically or geographically. Suffice it to say that here in 1973, in what one might call 'Western civilization', things seem to have reached a low ebb. We are brought up to believe that the first and only person to help is oneself; though it is permissible, if necessary, to help an old lady across the road and, should earthquakes strike, dig people out from under the rubble. The fact that we do all respond in times of crisis surely shows that the ability, even the need, to help one another, is lurking there. Unfortunately the opportunities to use it have become more and more limited – social workers are posted along every road in Samaria these days. Faced with these professional 'helpers' we shrug ourselves into a comfortable apathy. *They* are looking after things. On top of this, somehow, somewhere or other in the recent past, outside times of crisis, it became a positive embarrassment to be seen helping someone else. This seems to be clearly rooted in two important features of our society, individualism and competition. The ruthlessness which characterizes the business world is becoming more and more a feature of the social world. Thankfully it hasn't laid a grip on anywhere near all of us completely, but it is there, gnawing away. Such dehumanizing forces as the motor-car and the high-rise flat are well-publicized factors of a worsening situation. They isolate people from one another.

So we have modern man who believes that people, like businesses, must fight for survival against one another – which means they can't help each other. He drives in his car past a road accident. The thought of stopping just to *offer* help may not even occur to him. For the police deal with the law, the doctors deal with the dead wife and dead husband, the social workers with the bereaved children. After all, he thinks to himself, it's so much more economical to have people to deal with these things, for if he stopped he might become involved and miss that important appointment, ruin that valuable free time, for rest and relaxation are important to ensure a good fighting spirit on Monday morning. Before the good Samaritan came along, plenty of others passed by.

An extreme picture, perhaps? Well, it certainly isn't Women's Lib which stops us from giving up our seat on the commuters' train. It is just that the desire to help is steadily being crushed out of us. We feel silly if we help, or rather, if we are seen to help. We are making an exhibition of ourselves. That is because we are educated and indoctrinated to think only of ourselves. And those professionals who are caring for the problems of society are actually fanning these devouring fires of apathy.

While it is often tempting to say that if we abandon the economic rat-race and return to a village-style existence we shall be socially a good deal more civilized, and while it may well be true, we hope to look at the situation a little more realistically.

These days helping one another often comes down to some financial transaction. It is true to say that 'charity' is big business indeed. We may feel moved to toss a couple of bob to the old boy outside Charing Cross station, but as to speaking to him. . . . And if someone sceptically points out 'he's probably going to spend it on another pint', the whole situation becomes too embarrassingly complex to think about and we hurriedly thrust it out of mind.

In school after school that we have visited we are faced with this: young people raising money until the cows come home. Home by courtesy of Shelter, of course. It is true that hard cash is often needed, but the danger is that our younger generation grow up equating 'help' with 'cash'. Most of the things we describe later in this book have nothing to do with money. Doubling the old-age pension is essential but it won't eliminate loneliness. Plenty of young people know that, and that kind of understanding is what we are aiming for, rather than a knowledge of how to organize a sponsored walk.

The roots of this money-raising lie in the sort of service which we would call 'Victorian philanthropy' or 'The Lady Bountiful' approach. For there were, and regrettably still are many, 'the poor and needy', for whom hard cash, or some physical manifestation of it, like a bowl of soup with a crust of bread, or a supplementary benefit, was the answer. The Department of Health and Social Security has largely replaced the soup kitchens run by those Edwardian and Victorian philanthropists. So charity isn't just big business – it's a veritable institution! What hasn't been taken over by the Department is left to philanthropy – but a philanthropy characterized by money-raising machines. School children who raise money for these charities have, like ourselves, only very sketchy ideas about what the charity does with the money. So they come to the realization 'it's the money that counts, not the thought'.

Even in more practical forms of service the 'money' syndrome occurs. If you ask a school what they do besides raising money for charity, the answer is very often 'Christmas parcels for the old folk'. This, it is true, is a step in the right direction, and there is no doubt that the parcels are welcomed. But the effort soon comes down to getting a list of addresses of lonely old people. In a similar way 'collecting clothes for children in care' is liable to be reduced in the minds of many youngsters to an effort for kids in rags living in austere surroundings and banging spoons on the table for more gruel. Highly educational.

Thus, community service by young people in the 1970s has, as one of its roots, this old philanthropic idea of the rich giving to the poor. Even that has been dehumanized by the mindless raising of money for mysterious charities, at home and abroad, while the 'soup kitchen' effort continues with the collection and distribution of Christmas parcels and bundles of clothes. In such a way we cause future generations to make the same kind of depersonalized response to helping others as we make ourselves. The point missed is that if we help each other in a personal, face-to-face way, that is *real* philanthropy.

Even so, by the late 1950s some well-known schools, mostly in the private sector, were beginning to give some encouragement to their pupils to offer practical service to others. But from the outset in these schools, and the many others who subsequently joined their ranks, the activity was called *voluntary* service. Again we have to go back to the Victorian era for an explanation of that 'voluntary'. For philanthropy was voluntary, and for the conscience to be eased fully, as great a sacrifice of one's own time and effort as possible was necessary. You have to suffer to salve your conscience. For young people in the mid-twentieth century this meant that you weren't really giving service unless it ate into your free time, the ultimate in conscience-salving being foregoing 'Top of the Pops' in order to visit the old folks' home, five miles away, in a raging snowstorm.

Of course, you had to make up your own mind to 'serve', perhaps encouraged a little by stirring talks about Florence Nightingale and Albert Schweitzer in morning assembly. But we should bring this 'voluntary' picture up to date, for in many schools 'voluntary' is no longer quite the word. We have often been asked to talk to the pupils involved in voluntary service, and have found that, it being Thursday afternoon, or whatever the appropriate day, it is considerably earlier than 4 p.m. So voluntary service has made some headway. It is no longer confined to after school and week-ends, but actually goes on in school time. Are the books slammed shut at a prescribed hour for an assault to be made on the local community? Have the 'University Honours' boards in the school hall been replaced by 'Outstanding Service to the Community' rolls of honour?

These thoughts are disturbed by the tramp of boots and the bellows of a Sergeant-Major from the direction of the basketball courts. The reality, of course, is that 'voluntary service' is an alternative activity to games, CCF and orienteering. So when we are led to the audience we find a small, often faintly weedy-looking, collection: the group who opt out of the more exciting athletic activities to do voluntary service. No, that description is unfair. Many have chosen this, and, still sacrificing, given up the chance to play their favourite sport or enjoy the camaraderie of the army. So in some ways things haven't changed. It frequently turns out that voluntary service has a poor name among those not involved: 'You won't catch me among the do-gooders!'; 'It's just the religious types who go in for it'; 'That's so boring – talking to old people all afternoon? You must be joking!'

So really the service isn't strictly voluntary. But gasps of horror are the reaction when we suggest that there should be more of a place – a bigger place, involving more pupils – for service. Tentatively we ask whether community service couldn't be something involving, well, let's be frank, *all* of the pupils, say? 'Why not put it on the timetable?' we suggest blithely.

There are two reactions to this question. First there's the old argument about service as sacrifice: 'While the school gives every encouragement, the desire to serve others can't be enforced. Why, the whole essence of service is that it is voluntary.' But before someone asks a further embarrassing question about how that statement fits in with the games/CCF/orienteering/service model, which implies that one of them *has* to be done, comes the second reaction: . . . 'and besides, you have to realize that our duty here is to get these boys through their O and A-levels, and with the pressure on university places becoming even greater, we'd be failing in our duty if we started carving whole hunks out of our timetable for – what was it you called it – community service? The parents wouldn't hear of it.' So the twentieth-century academic rat-race and the remnants of nineteenth-century middle-class philanthropy combine to produce a small audience of boys and girls for a Thursday afternoon talk.

Before proceeding to the way in which less well-known establishments tackle their community service, it is worth noting that in 1958 Alec Dickson founded Voluntary Services Overseas (VSO). This organization enabled many young people to work overseas on a voluntary basis. 'Doing VSO' involved little sacrifice, for leaving school one had the chance to wait for a year before going to college or starting work. The founding of VSO did much also to stimulate voluntary service in Britain, for schools recognized the value, educationally, of service to others, but realized that only a few would get the chance because VSO had to be selective. So schools began voluntary service groups to enable pupils to give service to their own local community. Paying lip-service to the 'educational value', it became the Thursday afternoon activity we have described.

Now the plot thickens. For a group of educationists, long, long ago, were looking for new things to put into the school timetable, things which had 'educational value'. The group was called the Central Advisory Council for Education (England), and they were brought together from March 1961 onwards by the Minister of Education, Lord Eccles:

To consider the education between the ages of thirteen and sixteen of pupils of average or less than average ability who are or will be following full-time courses either at schools or in establishments of further education. The term education shall be understood to include extra-curricular activities.[2]

The report, which the group published in 1963, was entitled *Half our Future*, for the pupils they were considering

constitute, approximately, half the pupils of our secondary schools; they will eventually become half the citizens of this country, half the workers, half the mothers and fathers and half the consumers . . .

In the way of all reports, however, it came to be called after the group's chairman, the Newsom Report. The children that the report covered came to be known as 'Newsom children'. A whole range of recommendations were made in the report, covering everything from the need to raise the school-leaving age – a recommendation finally carried out in 1972 – to better courses, better buildings, better trained teachers, better equipment.

The value of community service was mentioned in various places in the report. The evidence heard by the group suggested that prefect and monitor systems were by no means the only way of creating opportunities to exercise leadership:

A few heads suggest that a less authoritarian organization may be more appropriate to present-day concepts, and are anxious to find ways in which older pupils can be given personal responsibility. One way may lie through community service projects.[3]

But it was not merely opportunities for leadership that community service offered:

There is a double value, in the usefulness of the service itself, and in the satisfaction of the boys and girls concerned in doing a real job. The pupils who are restive and feel themselves outgrowing the interests of a purely internal school society may especially respond to these more adult responsibilities.[4]

To these apparent educational merits of community service – leadership opportunity, satisfaction in doing a real job, and adult responsibility – the report added others: status and team-work:

Anything which can serve to emphasize the status of the older pupils is to be welcomed ...

It may be that learning to become a reliable member of a group of equals is, for many, a better general preparation for life.... Community service projects appear to offer particularly satisfying possibilities.[5]

These brief extracts are the most important references in the report to community service and the educational value which accrues from it. What happened as a result of them? Many schools took a good deal of notice of what the Newsom Report had to say, and from 1963 onwards increasing numbers of secondary moderns and comprehensives began to incorporate community service in the timetables of the early leavers.

The traditionalists were struck with horror. All the essential characteristics of what they in their grammar and public schools called 'voluntary' service were missing from this new pattern. Timetabling? That makes it compulsory. Where was the sacrifice? Here was a fundamental dilemma: the 'voluntarists' were leaving the spiritual and moral development of their pupils to chance. They were leaving the motivation to come from pupils' hearts while the school concerned itself with academic development. Yet the Newsom Report, in talking of spiritual and moral development was saying:

A school which takes its responsibility seriously will not just leave to chance the working out of its influence over its pupils. It will have a policy....[6]

Part of the policy, naturally, was community service, and many hundreds of schools, in the years after 1963, took up that policy. Like it or not, the Newsom children, the 'early-leavers', were going to be of practical service to others.

What then do we find today, when visiting schools where community service is on the timetable? The following is a factual account of a visit to a boys' secondary modern school in the London area.

Arriving at the school, we were conscious of a generally run-down atmosphere. The buildings were neither new nor old, reflecting very much the character of the local housing. The audience were the fourth year, or rather the lower-ability part of it, and they were crammed, about a hundred of them, into one average-sized classroom. On arrival we realized that something akin to a riot was in progress. This was no place for the faint-hearted. A teacher made the introduction, shouting in order to be heard, and when he mentioned the title of the talk – 'Helping Others' – there fell a deathly hush, broken only by someone in the front row throwing back his head and saying 'God Almighty!' Giving the talk was well-nigh impossible, for not only did the audience show no reaction at all to hearing of the problems of others, and what they could do about them, it was almost as if they didn't understand. Matters weren't helped by the several teachers prowling around continuously, administering blows with rulers and hefty textbooks. We never gave a talk called 'Helping Others' again.

So, to begin with, there is a motivation problem among these children, for they neither understand the problems nor appreciate what they can do. A pity, since they clearly have no less social maturity than the academic streams. But where there is compulsion without motivation, disaster lurks. There always seems to be a character at a teachers' conference who is eager to tell the rest of the audience about a community-service scheme stopped in its tracks by Jim or Fred who stole money from the old lady he visited. No need to ask if Jim or Fred were 'volunteers' or Newsom kids! To counter such problems, more supervision was needed, so that Jim or Fred were always under somebody's watchful eye. But more supervision needs more teachers, who weren't forthcoming. Community service got stuck, its potential, educational and social, left untapped.

What kind of work are the Newsom children doing? Frankly, it is generally appallingly unimaginative, partly due to the fact that too many schools have stopped short of the mark. They hesitate to provide 'real jobs', real leadership opportunities, real adult responsibility, preferring instead to water down community service to what they consider manageable proportions. Result: children visit the elderly, dig their gardens, do a little work in institutions, and other odd jobs. As we say later, the fact that community service has got stuck at such a mundane level isn't all due to teachers who lack the courage to really give kids a chance to show what they are worth. It's also due to the reluctance of others to accept the services of young people, for the 'voluntary service' activities have also got stuck at this same level.

In spite of the chasm of difference between voluntary and compulsory, therefore, the one has not 'proved' itself over the other by developing bigger and better projects. Another similarity is that in secondary moderns and comprehensives community service makes as little impact on the academic mainstream as it does in grammar and public schools. The truth is that the majority of teachers want to teach 'their' subject to children receptive to that subject. Each teacher of each subject protects his or her patch, the children and the curriculum, from outside interference. This is a pattern of which we shall see more later, in other contexts, for it is typical of 'professionalism'.

But back to 1962 for a moment. In that year Alec Dickson left V S O to turn his attention to problems in Britain. He had realized that the problems of the twentieth century weren't just to be found in the jungles of Africa and Asia, they were alive and well and living in Britain too. In a way which is educative for all of us, he acted first and worried about committees and organization afterwards. He founded Community Service Volunteers (C S V), operating in much the same way as V S O at first. But it was to the remand homes, psychiatric hospitals, Cheshire Homes, gypsy communities – the list is endless – that the eighteen-year-old school-leaver volunteers went, rather than to teach, nurse and 'help' overseas. Ten years later C S V were filling one thousand projects a year with one thousand volunteers. But one policy in particular became C S V's trademark: 'We never reject anyone – do you?'[7] They meant that there was no selection procedure for volunteers, for to help other people is a right, not a privilege. The proof of this thesis is in the number of emotionally unstable young people, borstal boys and blind kids joining the school leavers and young graduates in CSV's waiting room. But we think they would all agree that they are still privileged. For though the opportunity of helping others on £2·50p per week is there, £2·50p per week is quite a sacrifice! On the other hand, more realistic pocket-money cannot be offered, for like most bodies with charitable status, CSV never has quite enough money to go round.

At the same time as Alec Dickson was commencing operations on this kind of national scale from his kitchen table, Anthony Steen was involving East End kids in helping the elderly at a local level. So his Task Force came into being in London, the second major form of 'organized' community service. By 1971 there were ten Task Force centres in London, each serving a whole borough. It was clear to Anthony Steen that this kind of organized service could work outside London, and so, in 1968 the Young Volunteer Force Foundation (YVFF) began, and 'centres' sprang up here and there throughout the country, in Cwmbran, Stoke, Newcastle, etc. Steen's YVFF became the third organization, with a head office in London and centres where local authorities could be convinced of the need for them, to involve local young people in local tasks. Gradually the philanthropy/sacrifice aspect of service died out. Anthony Steen was more concerned with 'practical involvement' by young people as an alternative to the expression of frustration in anti-social ways – gang violence and vandalism. This was therapy rather than philanthropy. But in the 1970s the YVFF centres turned down a dead-end street. Therapy for the young was changed to therapy for whole communities and 'community development' became the YVFF watchword: stimulating whole communities to help themselves. All right if you believe outside workers can effect that stimulation. We feel that centres for community development already exist in the communities, and that given the chance they will effect community development from within. Given the chance.

Ah! How the organizations multiplied! For while CSV Task Force and YVFF fought for the money which occasionally circulated from the big trusts and foundations and local authorities and government departments, another form of organized community service was burgeoning all over the country, reflecting the Task Force model in London. The names which you find today tell their own story: Young Volunteers of Merseyside, Birmingham Young Volunteers, Youth Action Halifax, Bexley Unit for Service by Youth (BUSBY), Action Clacks (Clackmannanshire). Some of these resulted from local authority initiatives, from the education or youth-service departments. Others came from voluntary origins from Councils of Social Services (which generally exist to coordinate the adult voluntary bodies). Some of the groups were run, in the early years, by long-term volunteers from CSV, later replaced by paid local authority staff.

Part of the reason for this 'volunteer boom' came from within the schools. For many Youth Action or Task Force organizations became involved in almost contractual relationships with local secondary schools. What a perfect arrangement! The hard-pressed teachers, fed up with, or daunted by the thought of running around town supervizing the Newsom children at their community-service work, and, worse still, trying to fix up projects in the local community for kids to actually do the good works, heaved a sigh of relief. Task Force would do it for them. 'One hundred and sixty-four schools were involved and forty-five had put Task Force on the curriculum ...'[8] That was the Task Force scene in London in early 1969. For community service read Task Force. Up and down the country the Youth Actions were doing the same thing. They looked after the children, found the projects, even did a bit of teaching in the school itself to back up the practical work outside school with follow-up sessions in the classroom. In return they received payment from the local education authority. So community service became a neat package deal.

There is one obvious danger in this kind of arrangement. The teachers were opting out of participation in an important learning process, and doing it quite happily, because organizing community service is a difficult and time-consuming business, which they had neither the time nor the 'knowledge' (about who does what in the community) to perform. In fact in some ways we must positively commend the attitude of the teachers. They were quite happy to allow 'non-professionals' – the Youth Action staff – to enter the teaching game, and such attitudes are few and far between in professional fields. But it was an attitude assumed because it took care of the early leavers for a while, not because it would encourage outsiders into schools. There are plenty of schools who do not have such an organization in the area, and we feel that they are lucky rather than unlucky, for development seems to us to be easier without the complication of a local organization for 'young volunteers'.

There is a phrase which has been kicking around for some years now – 'community service and the curriculum'. To many teachers this has meant 'timetabled community service for the early leavers' or, as we have seen, 'Task Force for early leavers'. That is, the lower streams in secondary moderns and comprehensives have 'community service' on their timetable, perhaps with a whole afternoon reserved for the subject. It may be the practical aspect of their 'social studies' or 'social education'.

To us and other heretics, this does not make sense. We believe that 'community service and the curriculum' means something quite different: it means exploring the ways in which all the present, established school subjects (i.e. the curriculum) can contribute to a young persons' knowledge about society and its problems, and by doing so provide a springboard for action. Not only the subjects, but an individual's skills, hobbies and interests (i.e. the personal curriculum) can be made relevant to the community in this way. We do not intend to document this approach in detail here; we shall do that later. We mention it because clearly the presence of a local young volunteer organization, running community-service work for schools on a package basis, will, under the present arrangement, prevent the development of real 'community service and the curriculum'. For real community service and the curriculum means that all the teachers will be involved and not just one hard-pressed social studies, social education or religious education teacher.

All the organizations, both national and local, have a method of operation generally known as the 'clearing house' system. The organization finds out the needs, then finds volunteers to fill them. Note the priority. The needs come first, the volunteers later. Of course, it may well work the other way round. Task Force in London may have contracted to occupy thirty children for a particular school and find themselves under some pressure to locate jobs for them to do. Likewise C S V, sending out long-term volunteers all over the country, are continually worried by the thought that they will have too many volunteers for the projects available. A situation arises where the needs and aspirations of the young people come rather a poor second to the needs of the 'projects'. So 'sacrifice' crops up again, for the young person must do the job he gets, regardless of his own unique talents and abilities.

Finally there is the danger that the simple business of helping someone else will be associated with 'joining the organization'. This danger is inherent in 'organizing' anything, inherent in giving young people, or anybody else, the impression that the only way you can help is to join up. In this kind of attitude lies the 'they will deal with it' apathy which has become a common feeling for all of us. Social work is associated with the local authority social services department and we feel that they are the people who take care of our neighbour's problems. In this case we can't even join up, for this is a professional body. So we don't think to offer our help. It would be a pity to associate community service work with a new 'them' (Task Force, Youth Action groups, etc.). Because 'they' organize it, children may not realize that they can help without joining 'them'. This problem is very acute in the environmental field, where there is a plethora of organizations.

Regrettably, though in a very human way, organizations like to play the numbers game, partly to justify next year's local authority grant. More volunteers and more projects must always be sought; so the organization works towards status as an established institution and too often succeeds. Then it is a privilege to succeed in joining it. Privilege? That's come up before.

Some organizations turned up a different cul-de-sac from the one Anthony Steen chose for Y V F F. This was labelled 'training volunteers' and it is easy to see why they chose it. Frustrated at seeing young 'volunteers' pushed into the most meaningless and peripheral jobs because of their youthful inexperience, the organizations, quite logically, thought that the best way to improve the status of their young volunteers was to train them. For a time we thought that way too. The logic was that if you have a young volunteer who has had a dose of knowledge of, say, 'mental health', then he will make a 'better' volunteer, more acceptable to the institution concerned. Logical but wrong. The trained young volunteer represents even more of a threat to the professionals, those professionals whom the organizations were trying to persuade to accept the services of more young people. The training also began to make the young volunteers resemble the professionals. That was even worse.

And is training feasible for kids like those early leavers who suffered our talk on 'Helping Others'? Would it turn them on any more than our talk? Yet should they be excluded from the chance to serve because they don't want the chance to train?

No one saw these things more clearly than Alec Dickson, who held out all along against 'training' volunteers. No one saw it less clearly than Enterprise Youth, in Scotland, who continue to hold what they call 'training weekends' for volunteers. Like the businesses they increasingly reflected, the organizations wanted to create 'a good product'.

We must acknowledge that the 'volunteer boom' owes much to the organizations. But we hope that they will see the need for change in themselves, guarding against institutionalization and too little concern with the needs of young people, if the boom is to continue.

Meanwhile, back in the world of education.... The community service machine which had been set in motion by the Newsom Report received little further official help or seal of approval until 1968, when the Schools Council published its Working Paper no. 17 *Community Service and the Curriculum*. The Schools Council is a government-funded body, which concerns itself with the development of new curricula and new examination structures. It has made a great impact on educational practice. Working Paper no. 17 was produced with much help from Neil Paterson – i.e. he wrote the bulk of it – who ran C S V's Advisory Service for Schools. Formerly he had pioneered the development of the Voluntary Service Unit at Sevenoaks School, under the headmastership of L. C. Taylor.

The Schools Council were clearly none too sure about the reaction of schools to curricular community service. The Working Paper set out to argue a case for community service on the timetable, based on five years' experience since Newsom had favoured community service as part of the school curriculum. But Working Paper no. 17 began with a fine piece of 'please 'em all':

To translate into the curriculum what is voluntary and done out of school time may still continue to raise the question of whether the value of an activity diminishes if as a curriculum requirement it loses its voluntary aspect. To schools which have already brought such activity into the curriculum the distinction between what is voluntary and what is compulsory does not raise difficulties either of practice or philosophy. Some pupils have more interest in such work, others less, some are better at it, others are not so good. But these disparities appear to stem more from the normal variance between the attitudes and capacities of individual pupils (a variance which is revealed in all aspects of the curriculum) than from the imposition of newly conceived prescription.

If schools feel that they should know of the needs and troubles of their community at first hand, they will treat service to that community as a normal part of curricular activity; if other schools feel, as can be argued from the other side, that the aims of education require some protection, at least until a later age, of the pupil from the pressures and problems of the community, they will continue to regard service as essentially an out-of-school task.[9]

This business of protecting the pupil from the horrors of the world outside still rears its head from time to time. Quite often work in a psychiatric institution is ruled out because of the 'alarming things the children might see'. That this kind of protection leads not only to ignorance but frequently to prejudice hardly seems worth pointing out.

In some ways the working paper sought to draw on five years' worth of experience in the schools to provide some kind of ground-rules or blueprint. It was a useful document, although it only just resisted the temptation to talk about timetabling community service for the early leavers only.

Many schools think the fourth year is the most suitable time to begin a systematic programme of community service as a regular part of the timetable. By the fourth year, young people are beginning to look beyond the school and to think themselves into adult roles ... they can generally be trusted on their own outside school.... [They] are capable of developing sustained personal relationships....[10]

Was the aim simply to ease the consciences of teachers guilty of using community service to get rid of the fourth year? The above educational mumbo-jumbo was reassuring to them. But the reassurance could be qualified with straight talk:

But for some teachers community service is not an activity peculiarly appropriate to a particular age group ... community service work is not seen simply as a remedial activity for the fourth year.... The majority of schools have developed this work with the early school leaver; other, but fewer schools, provide time for this work both in the fifth and sixth forms....[11]

Aside from the 'who' question, some forward-looking points were raised about *real* curriculum-based community service:

Probably the first point where there will be contact between the community service programme and the rest of the curriculum will be in the practical subjects....[12]

Some brief suggestions were made as to how other subjects could relate, but perhaps the time was not yet ripe for the spread of community service through all the subjects of the curriculum.

Other educationists did take note of the idea, educationists who were concerned less with community service work, but rather with the realistic development of practical subjects. Two Schools' Council Research and Development Projects, concerned separately with 'Design and Craft' and 'Technology', saw the value of relating these disciplines to the community through service. Later we shall describe how schools in Llangefni, North Wales and Crewe found that there was more to craft than coffee tables and toast racks, through their contact with the Design and Craft project team. We shall also describe how the Technology project helped young people to clear up a canal. Three schemes out of many stimulated by the project teams.

Time to draw breath. We have tried to describe how the original 'voluntary' service, which still exists in many schools, was overtaken in the quantitative sense by 'compulsory' service by the early leavers. We have tried to describe the organization 'boom' as well as to create a composite picture of the way things look today. But it is the school picture which is our major concern. Here service is still unnatural. It is something which you think you should do, so you volunteer, or something which you find yourself doing because it's on your timetable, just like maths and English. Now our whole thesis is that our communities are disintegrating in the social sense precisely because it is unnatural for us to help one another. Time, therefore, that schools, instead of merely reflecting society, even protecting children from it, made service a natural activity. One of the ways this can be done is by making the whole school curriculum concerned with the needs and problems of the community and the individuals who comprise it. Every school subject and every school activity has something to contribute to this, and every school pupil must be affected. This last point is crucial. Maybe we have to live with examinations and the academic struggles that lead to them. That need not prevent this change. Making the curriculum relevant in every subject to community needs and problems is a prospect which will daunt the educational reformers of the Schools Council. But since Working Paper no. 17 nothing has happened. Time, we feel, that something did.

We might call our approach 'Community Education'.[13] That is, education about the community, for the community's ultimate benefit. As we shall see, more is needed than giving a little social ambiance to the curriculum. What is also needed, and 'Community Education' would be incomplete without it, is the end of 'service to others', with its implied condescension to the poor and needy, and a new 'service for the community'. For this to occur schools will have to change more than their curriculum. They will have to change their whole function. But then the education will begin.

The school-leaving age has finally been raised to sixteen. The early leavers have become the not-so-early leavers. But the traditions die hard, and we strongly suspect that the new fifth-year leavers will get the same dose as before:

> ... contact may be achieved with the work and active life of the various social services ...[14]

Let us not end our description there. We must say, fairly and squarely, that too few of the reports and organizations really take account not just of the needs of young people, but also of their real abilities, not least of which are their energy, enthusiasm and enterprise. The Schools' Council have a housewife on one of their interminable committees. Why not a pupil? No doubt the answer to that is that organizations are concerned with the problems – old people, the mentally handicapped – which forces them to put young people in second place. Nonsense. The kids are a problem, or rather have a big problem because we give them no chance to contribute on terms they understand and accept.

The Aves Committee Report on *The Voluntary Worker in the Social Services*, published in 1969, and largely ignored thereafter, thank goodness, had this comment on community service work by children:

> The social services must give priority to the needs of their clients, and cannot see them regarded primarily as teaching material.
>
> We are also concerned about the effects on children themselves of being involved in community service ...
>
> ... to include community service in compulsory education, or to do more than encourage spontaneous participation by children not only negates the concept of service, but may defeat its own aims.
>
> ... we have very considerable reservations about ... the encouragement by education authorities of community service as an educational activity within the curriculum; and about the expressed desire of at least one of the organizations providing opportunities for service by young people to see it enormously increased.[15]

It goes without saying that most of the members of the Aves Committee came from the field of social work. What they are saying is – off our patch, educationists. And both the social workers and the educationists forgot all about the kids.

Then there was the Seebohm Report, and the subsequent reorganization of the statutory provision of social services. This looked more promising, and the reorganization took place from 1970 onwards.

> New types of voluntary organizations are emerging – increasingly characterized by the youthfulness of their members and the radical nature of their criticism of the existing services ...
>
> The (social services) department must include volunteers in its plans, and it will have to show, in the training of new staff, the important role of the volunteer ...[16]

Good idea: train your staff, not your volunteers. Not so good: here we are three years later and whatever happened to that fine thought about volunteers complementing professionals (we'd prefer to see it the other way round, with professionals complementing volunteers). 'Giving and receiving service for the whole community'? Sorry kids, you missed out again.

We haven't mentioned many other things. There is the 'service' element in the Duke of Edinburgh's Award Scheme, for example, still reflecting the sacrificial aspect of service in its rules. And then there is IBM – that's right, the computer firm – and their 'Trident' project with schools, which includes community service, work experience and leisure/adventure activities. This mammoth PR exercise was conducted according to efficient business principles, meaning that IBM bought themselves what they considered to be the most expert advice available on community service. Why didn't they talk to a few kids?

Most recently there was the report presented to the

Department of the Environment in 1972 on 'The role of voluntary organizations and youth in the environment.' Entitled *Fifty Million Volunteers,* it contained some good thinking, but its main argument was that volunteers must be more and better organized. In contrast, our main thesis is that people need less organization and a lot more power, young people in particular. If power and participation are to flourish they must be freed of this 'organization' noose, and who cares about efficiency? What we want is a labour-intensive social system, not an efficient, economical, unpeopled one.

One dilemma that has now struck the whole young volunteer movement, volunteers and organizers, is the 'gap-plugging' problem. Many volunteers and their organizers, and the *Fifty Million Volunteers* report agreed with them, feel that some jobs shouldn't be performed by volunteers, because by doing them they are just propping up an inadequate system of social care, and therefore perpetuating it. So pull out, they say, and expose the system and if possible use the experience as a lever to exert political pressure, at the national or local level. Here is an example of this type of dilemma. Are CSV right to send in a whole team of volunteers to work in a psychiatric hospital? The volunteers and the staff at CSV who support them realize that the hospital is a loathsome place, and the volunteers see themselves as being there because the 'system' can't afford or attract proper staff.

The situation is a complex one, but on balance we find ourselves unmoved by the 'we must not plug gaps' brigade. We are in favour of the community running its own affairs, in institutions as elsewhere. If you are an anti-gap-plugger it invariably means that you are in favour of increased provision by government and local authority, which is opposed to the self-help idea. Gaps which need plugging are opportunities – opportunities for the community to be of service directly. Every gap plugged by any individual is a foot in the door of the institution, and every foot in the door is a step towards community take-over, towards 'we'll do it, not them'. And once the community is within, then the isolated institution will be destroyed and replaced by community care. Community care will not be enforced from above, as reports and governments may like to think. It will arrive with a vengeance when the community itself sees inside the institutions, unblinkered by professionals, and knows their weaknesses for itself. At the same time its own fears of handicap and the unknown are overcome, and the hostel for the mentally handicapped, or the handicapped lodger, become realities. We never met a young person who has worked in a mental hospital who didn't believe in community hostels for the mentally handicapped. But the more provision we have, the more professionals we shall have and the more professionals there are, the harder it becomes for the community to look after its own. So if one comes to the point, as C S V did in the psychiatric hospital, when one suddenly realizes that the institution is actually depending on volunteers, treat it as a victory, not a defeat.

Our contact with young people has shown us that they are more responsive to our ideas than those who purport to represent their interests, or the interests of those the young people wish to serve, and it is that single fact that we care about most. The short, happy life of the young volunteer will end very soon, unless we sweep aside those organizations, often listed in the 'We are grateful to the following for submitting evidence ...' sections of all the relevant reports, who think they know best. Whether in education, the youth service, the social services, one of these organizations we have mentioned, or elsewhere, they are the problem. They are more of a problem than the social problems they are supposed to deal with, because they are not giving young people the chance to respond as they want to. Are they afraid of what the young might do to the society they have created? Do they fear active young citizens?

BEEF-STEAK ON THE WARD
LOOK GORGEOUS IS THERE ANYTHING I CAN DO TO HELP?
MATRON

NEXT MORNING.....
IDEA
VISITING HOUR

2 Institutions

What prospects do our institutions of education and welfare present to those who wish to participate in them? We would like to discuss this before describing the work young people are doing in institutions.

Institutions are exclusive places: you belong or you don't; you are an insider or an outsider; you are in the know or you are not. Schools demonstrate this exclusivity. In a time when we all have to go to school, those who attend school belong to it; those who have left don't belong any more. The return visit to alma mater is a puzzling and rather empty experience.

Institutions are not just worlds in themselves but laws unto themselves. They make their own rules and create their own standards. School rules often contrast sharply with those of non-school world. Perhaps school uniform must be worn at all times, or silence may be the golden rule, or running in the corridor the cardinal sin.

TEACHER: I couldn't allow these girls out of school to do community service in school time – this is a garrison town, you must realize. They'd be picked up by some soldier in no time.

Q: But isn't that just as likely to happen to them after school, and at weekends?

TEACHER: Ah yes, but that's nothing to do with me, is it?

Other kinds of institutions also make rules which are puzzling and frustrating to both outsider and insider. 'No children during visiting hours' – in a maternity hospital; 'Patients are only allowed out if they hold a permission card' – from a mental hospital.

Anyone who has visited a school as an outsider has noticed

this club atmosphere, the feeling of being on forbidden territory. Parents notice it when they attend parents' evenings; students at evening classes notice it even more. The notices on the boards, the pictures on the wall are cryptic and alien, they don't belong to the visitor. The hospital visitor, the caller at the 'department', feel lost and uncomfortable too, and the institution actively fosters this feeling, so that the outsider feels that this place is no place for him. Even to those who never enter, the institution radiates an ivory-tower mystique. Sometimes it leads to suspicion. Residents of the Potteries have long referred to the University of Keele as 'the Kremlin on the Hill'. Often it leads to awe and reverence from the outsider for the institution. They obey the rules and swallow their awkward feelings, thinking that 'they' know what's best, 'they' know what they are doing. Any attempt to de-institutionalize must therefore have two objectives: to change the attitude of the outsiders as well as that of the insiders.

It has always been in the interest of the professional to prevent the world at large from gaping through his classroom window, from prying into his client's affairs, from upsetting his routine. Otherwise totally unqualified people might start imagining that they can do his job just as well as he can! So these feelings of awe are actively cultivated. The professional asserts himself and then builds his fortification as a protection from the layman.

Besides promoting this alien atmosphere, the institution makes cunning use of two further weapons against outside attack. Firstly, jargon. The professional delights in bamboozling the outsider with the jargon of his trade. The social worker talks of the importance of confidentiality in casework, the matron refers to the highly particularized needs of the terminal, long-stay geriatrics; the nursing auxiliary tells that little can be done with the multi-handicapped sub normal patient: 'She's a C and C case, I'm afraid'.[17] Teachers talk in the same way: team-teaching, vertical integration of studies, remedial workshops. All of these are quite simple things, but the expressions confuse and mystify the outsider. And eventually the conscious becomes unconscious and the message is the same: 'Hands off.'

The superman who penetrates the jargon will surely fall scaling the final wall of hierarchy and personal relationship. Beyond this the institution hums and throbs, or creaks and groans. Hierarchies are like fat, solid trees – you can easily hide behind them. The awkward outsider can be passed from person to person, up and down the hierarchy, until he becomes exhausted and gives up. Whoever you want to see is tracked down only with the utmost perseverance, and once you find him he's out, or he's left, or 'we are in the throes of a major reorganization.'

Gathering together a collection of school head-teachers to discuss the value of community service to young people doesn't do any good at all. It's up to the staff, they say, and if a staff member offers to take up the responsibility, well and good. Gathering together a collection of teachers would therefore seem to be the answer? Oh, no; it's the head and deputy head who allocate the timetable, and anyway majority time for the major subjects has to be put in first. Not only are head-teachers more powerful (or are they?) than teachers, but some teachers are more powerful than others. Curiouser and curiouser. The pupils themselves are in an odd situation. Theoretically part of the hierarchy – in our view at the top, but generally considered the bottom – yet they have no status and rights, like the outsider. In that state lies our great hope.

A network of personal relationships permeates and surrounds the hierarchical shield to give added protection. Chinks in the armour are closed in this way. The personal relationships protect the institution in two quite different ways. If all else fails the professionals can link together and support one another to create a formidable barrier. Conversely, though just as expedient, the instructions and advice of colleagues can be ignored or rejected for no better reason than a personal feud, or an assumed one. Change can be resisted equally effectively by either mechanism.

In these ways the institution seeks to protect itself, its property and its status, not just against the layman, but also against surprise attacks from other institutions, though fairly solid ground rules have long since been agreed. Social Services has nothing to do with Education, and vice versa. It is not so much a question of the directors of relevant authorities not knowing one another, for they are unimportant; it manifests itself in a complete lack of contact between teachers and area social workers. This is more serious. Though dealing with the same people, they have tacitly agreed that they have no need to work together. Although a head-teacher may have contact with the local probation officer, the teachers who are, they fondly imagine, closest to the children do not foster links with someone who is not in their business. On top of this principle of demarcation is the notion which institutions hold that *they* are the only ones who care about 'it', or are qualified to do anything about 'it' – their problem. Of all facets of the institution this is perhaps the most nauseating, since it is reason in itself to justify the rejection of the outsider.

Here is an example of such a rebuff. A teacher is initiating a community service scheme in his school and realizes that his children will not appreciate hypothetical notions about the need to help other people. So he decides to find some actual jobs which he can offer to his class. Out he goes into the community, and his travels will eventually bring him to an institution. Let us imagine him for the moment, having penetrated the veneers of hierarchy and relationships, having overcome his discomforts at not being in the 'know', having put aside the strong emanations that 'they' are capable of dealing with things, face to face with the person 'responsible'.

TEACHER: I've come to ask whether any of my pupils could help out here. We're introducing a scheme of community service at my school and . . .

PROFESSIONAL: What makes you think we need help here? We manage very well on our own. Would you like to take a look around?

We have seen that one already, but worse is to come.

TEACHER: I'm quite prepared to take your word for it. Let me put it differently, because I don't want you to think that I'm criticizing the valuable work you do. You see, as a teacher I'm concerned with educating my pupils and I feel that community service is not so much a way my children can help others, as a way others can help them. I want my pupils to see and understand the problems which other people face, and to develop certain skills which they can't learn in school but only through such practical work. That's really why I've come here.

PROFESSIONAL: Education is none of my business. I'm concerned with the care of the inmates here. You have to realize that it takes highly trained and qualified staff to look after these peoplc. We can't have your children here, whatever the reason.

The message is clear: 'Hands off'.

The British have an unjustified pride in their welfare state. We have allowed it to create institutions which take responsibility away from the people, and the process of delegating to the institutions our responsibility for one another leads to the gradual erosion of our own need and desire to do so. We become passive and atrophied. Most distressing, the activity which characterizes a new generation of young volunteers is faced with the status quo – establishments which control the function they want to share and which actively encourage passivity and ignorance amongst their ranks.

We once visited a PE teacher who had been asked by his local authority adviser to give us some guidance as to how PE lessons could relate to human need. *He* asked *us* what we had in mind. We pointed out that *he* was the expert, not us, but, as a starter, couldn't some of his lessons be devoted to devising games for handicapped children, or exercises for arthritics? Couldn't these be tried out at the local special school? The teacher had evidently expected this for he had prepared his answer, and we were consoled by the fact that we hadn't come far to hear it: 'There is no point in getting the boys to do that – it has been done already! There are books on the subject, and some colleges offer special courses to train teachers specializing in the physical education of the handicapped. These trained people can do a far better job at a special school than our boys can.' This formed the basis of his side of the conversation. We argued that the discovery of the problems faced by the handicapped was an important part of a child's education as a citizen, and that skill in this subject could be shared in a practical way with others. But his respect for the institution, the professional, the trained and qualified, was unshakeable. Here was a 'passivist'.

He showed us out, and in the corridor we passed a pupil from the class we had just caused him to miss: 'Well, Paul, what's the answer to the question I set you?' asked the PE teacher. 'For how many offences is an indirect free kick awarded?' Surely every trained and highly qualified referee in the country knows that already? Why bother?

Over the past years arguments have waxed and waned over how we should teach children to read, and what we should do about 'adult illiteracy'. Regrettably, and this is again characteristic of the institution, the *method* becomes overwhelmingly more important than the *result*. The social worker argues for casework against personal involvement; the teacher of reading argues the case for traditional methods against approaches based on psychiatry.

In the case of reading, parents have actually been led to believe that they must leave it to teachers to instruct their children. If they teach them to read they may be spoiling everything. They know best, they're trained, aren't they? A ridiculous situation arises:

Parents should be able to teach their children to read before they start school without feeling that they are trespassing on teachers' territory.[18]

But aside from this, what of our adult illiterates? The institutions of learning wash their hands of them so, fortunately, people can take over. The method is people, and the result is people.

There are over a million illiterates in this country; one in seven cannot fill in a normal form without help; one in ten cannot read a newspaper . . .

Very few local education authorities have tried to organize effectively for the need. Quite a number do not provide any tuition.[19]

The institution, therefore, has failed, although it may still try to protect itself, as it naturally doesn't want its inadequacies hanging out. But at least the outsider can penetrate, and he will be welcomed by someone as uncharacteristic of the professional as Cliff Edwards. This may not be the case and in that event how do young people concerned about illiteracy make a start?

Tackle the local education officer. Some local authorities will welcome help from volunteer teachers. . . . Do not make the mistake of waiting too long to hear from the Education Office – go and see them if you don't get a reply.[20]

He puts those who think the professional knows best immediately at their ease:

No, there is no need to worry about training. Just go in and teach. . . . I think our best teachers are a barrow boy, a barmaid and a trainee health visitor. They certainly beat me, anyway. On this matter on non-trained teachers more bilge is talked . . .[21]

These teachers – sixth formers, barrow boys and barmaids, – help each student individually.

Get the right atmosphere, use first names at all times and keep the fun bubbly. Thank heavens I don't have to tell young folk to be human and treat people as people.[22]

He concludes:

Don't give up just because a few clucking fuddy-duddies write up to the papers, to your school or to you and say that you are not doing things the right way. They aren't doing anything at all . . .

Within a few months one girl of twenty-three has reached a standard where she is enjoying George Orwell's *Animal Farm*; a woman of fifty-three has written her life story on seven pages, and a man of thirty-six has been able to tell his employers that he can read. He was promoted to foreman on the spot. Successes are by no means restricted to intelligent students. One young lady left an ESN school three years ago without being able to read more than her own name. In four months she has learnt to go through story after story in our tattered Wide Range Readers and is taking immense pride in her handwriting.[23]

The message is clear enough. Educating is not the prerogative of the school and people can assert their right to a share in it. In this case the institutions have washed their hands of a problem, thus allowing amateurs an 'easy' chance to tackle it. Even so, a scheme like this poses formidable difficulties to a group of young people undertaking it – permission, premises, equipment. The institution may preclude them by many means.

Many institutions possess equipment, resources and potential which their exclusiveness denies to the community. The community needs access to these resources if it is to explore its cooperative spirit, but the institution is all-powerful. Think of a university: buildings, playing fields and open spaces, bars and ballrooms, libraries and laboratories. The general public is denied access to this plenty, or feels too intimidated to venture in. Yet in the vacation the campus is deserted by the students and staff and it still belongs to them, it is still forbidden territory for the local community. Students and staff don't bother to try to change this state of affairs. The staff are part of the hierarchy, but why not the students? Their struggles seem to be directed towards becoming part of the hierarchy, never towards union with the outsider. We once suggested that all the resources of universities might be open to all at Christmas time. Nobody was very enthusiastic about an idea which had been successfully operated in Holland. We had hoped that some student union might tackle the scheme, but nobody ventured an initiative, though many expressed admiration.

We were not capable of seeing, it seemed, just how difficult to operate this scheme would be. Certainly many objections were raised to actual implementation: insurance of property, permission for use of this, that and other. All the sort of petty objections people get from institutions. We were disappointed in students' unions. They appeared, like pupils in schools, to be in an excellent position to effect change, but, though superficially enthusiastic, when it came to actively changing their institutions, they were afraid.

Schools have more limited resources but are also in a good position to focus community life. For the same reasons, however, these resources lie idle for much of the year. Playgrounds are closed in the holidays to the very kids who have to stay inside them during the term. It goes without saying that classrooms are closed, equipment locked away and libraries gather dust. The institution controls its own resources for its own ends. Hands off everyone else. Anybody who has tried to get a school re-opened in the holidays for, say a summer language project for immigrants will know how hard it is to locate the keys and secure the permission. The difficulties are enough to put off the most ardent. Even if the Headmaster and the Chief Education Officer agree, there is still a caretaker power to contend with. So the classroom, playgrounds and fields are useless as it is not considered in the school's interest if they were otherwise.

To say that students should open their universities, or at least, their unions, is not enough. To say that school children should seek access to empty schools is not enough. Young people do not see that they can do this, let alone that they should, because they are passive in their acceptance of institutional control. The important first step is to reject the passivity which is encouraged in them by their own institution. Students have achieved some success in terms of gaining representation on academic committees, senates and governing bodies, but now that they have obtained more influence in the university hierarchy, will they instigate communalization? Will they push for university facilities to be truly public property, available to anybody; will they demand courses which relate a little more realistically to present-day human need? If they don't, then the progress students have made towards some voice in their institutions was merely a step taken out of self-interest, the expression of a meaningless power struggle within the institution.

The institution provides a security, a familiar and tangible frame of reference to those who belong. In ripping this down we have to offer something better as security. We believe that a far more vivacious security, a living, growing sense of belonging, is offered by the people around us all the time, in our neighbourhood, our community. The institution provides a security for some, the community could offer it to all.

Right. Now to some rather more practical notions. From both within and without, these barriers which prevent the community from getting into their institutions must be destroyed. As we have said, we believe young people can be a most powerful force in effecting this change. All people should feel a part of the educating process and the caring processes, for all those who need care. They are at present part of these processes for little portions of their lives, and then they leave them behind. In just the same way that teaching is not the prerogative of a professional class, so neither is care of the mentally handicapped, the physically handicapped, the aged, the parentless and the like the right of a few. It is not in their best interest or the best interests of the community as a whole. You can counter this by saying that on the whole people have no real interest or desire to care about one another. Our theories are idealistic hopes. But hasn't the uncaring that exists been bred by institutions? And isn't it becoming more and more clear that these institutions, from school to mental hospital, are failing to perform their function? The function from which we have been excluded because they can do it all so much better. In particular, too many schools, despite the enormous resources of finance and manpower devoted to them, are failing to generate satisfied or integrated human beings. So preoccupied are schools with successes and competition that they show little inclination to try cooperation and a little interest in those who 'fail'.

For the moment we will try to see what can be learnt from the work of thousands of young people who have been engaged in community service in institutions, excluding the school itself. The latter deserves special attention.

In Glasgow in 1965 began the 'Hospital Scheme for Schools'. The aim of the scheme was to involve as great a number as possible of our fourteen to fifteen-year old pupils of average or less than average ability in giving a regular service to the community and at the same time to widen their field of education in a practical way.[24]

Naturally the Regional Hospital Board had to be approached first:

... to find out in the first place if the services of girls under fifteen years of age would be acceptable in the hospital.[25]

The Board agreed that they would be acceptable, but

... whether or not this idea could be put into operation, they warned, would of course depend on the matrons of the hospitals.[26]

There followed a meeting with the matrons and to their credit:

... twelve hospitals agreed to take part in the pilot scheme.[27]

It was decided that the girls would be provided with a suitable uniform and that many of the privileges and facilities open to nurses would be available to them, so that they could benefit from associating freely with the nursing staff. But

... it was obvious that with a scheme which demanded a pupil being out of school for four days within one month, only girls not involved in Scottish Certificate of Education could participate.[28]

However, the academically inclined were allowed to join in after their exams. It was also decided that parental permission was necessary for something which involved children being out of school.

The scheme began with twenty-two schools and twelve

hospitals. By 1970, forty-eight schools and twenty-two hospitals were involved, with each pupil working in a hospital for one or two days per week, over a maximum of a six-week period. The scheme undoubtedly operated highly successfully

. . . a number of matrons volunteered to accept more pupils.

But what did the work involve?

On the first morning pupils are escorted to the hospital unless it is within close proximity to the school. They meet the matron first of all, who talks to them generally about the hospital and shows them around some of the departments. After being equipped with their uniforms the girls are introduced to the sister of the ward in which they will help. The wards are carefully selected so that pupils are never confronted with dangerously ill patients or distressing cases. They are often delegated to the children's wards, when this is possible. Geriatric wards, too, have proved popular with the schoolgirls. The duties deputed to them are simple and are carried out under the watchful eyes of the nursing staff. Were you to visit a ward where a schoolgirl is on duty you might find her helping a nurse with the bedmaking, assisting in the service of meals, feeding a toddler or interesting it in play. Changing patients' drinking water, arranging flowers, attending to the comforts of the elderly, assisting with the bathing of new babies, are other duties which are carried out by pupils in the course of the day.[29]

It was necessary to formulate some fairly strict rules:

Pupils should be inspected before their visit to the hospital to ensure that they are clean and well-groomed. Long hair must be tied back. No pupil under fourteen-and-a-half years of age should participate. . . .[30]

The writer also mentioned that,

I met the Principal Teachers of Home Economics to brief them on their responsibilities regarding the selection of pupils.[31]

She concludes:

This kind of service makes a valuable contribution, not only to the development of the child, but also gives young people the feeling that they are able to contribute to the running of life in their community. . . .

Head teachers have commented on a number of occasions on the marked improvement of so many of their pupils after their term in hospital in regard to their self-confidence, personal appearance and ability to converse. They have gained, too, an understanding of the needs of others in a less fortunate position than themselves and it is not uncommon for the schoolgirls to return to the hospital to visit some of the geriatric patients and take them little gifts or offer their services on Saturdays and public holidays.[32]

All of these are worthwhile, though limited, educational objectives. But are we to accept this kind of approach as the way in which young people can make the most effective contribution? One must remember that this scheme began in 1965, soon after the publication of the Newsom Report, and we have already discussed the effect this had on service by young people. It is unnecessary for us to describe again the young people to whom this sort of experience was confined, but we repeat, Why only them? Was 'four days within one month' really too much for the academic pupils to be away from school? Why 'simple tasks' under 'watchful eyes'. Why all this condescending talk about whether girls were 'acceptable'?

There are three main questions to consider about the hospital scheme. What was the attitude of the institutions to these outsiders? What was the attitude of the young people to the professional staff? What did the young people accomplish?

The author and her colleagues in the schools realized from the start that they must tread carefully. The fact that they had to find out if the services of fifteen-year-old girls were 'acceptable' makes one feel slightly uncomfortable. There should be no question about it: if one believes in willingness, then acceptability is beyond question. But here there was a question, and it was passed on to the correct place in the hierarchy, the matrons, twelve of whom 'agreed to accept' the girls. What happened next? The girls became part of the system – uniforms and staff facilities. Untrained and unqualified, so naturally they were given the most pointless and unimportant jobs available; just read through that list of duties again. Besides this there were rules, selection procedures and an imposed system within which the young people worked.

The attitude of the institutions is mostly bad. Good only in that those twenty-two who participated undoubtedly took an enormous step forward, by acknowledging that education was their concern. Bad in that young people were simply absorbed into the system at the bottom and given tasks which can only be described as meaningless. The attitude of the young people we don't know, but we have met plenty on similar schemes, one of whom said, 'I felt that everything was being taken care of very nicely, and I was just there as a dogsbody.' What did the young people accomplish? Surely they were something new, refreshing in itself; they brought a human touch. They had the time to develop relationships with the patients, relationships which brought them back outside the scheme. But what they could accomplish was and always will be, restricted by the terms of reference imposed on them. And remember, they each had five or six weeks and that was their lot. If they learned and benefited from this experience in the way the author describes, how much more could they surely learn and benefit if the professional attitude was less imposing and condescending towards them? Such imposition and condescension can have worse results. Glasgow in 1970 also witnessed the wrecking of the Easterhouse Youth Club, by the very young people whom it served. If only the club had been *by* them and not just *for* them, built and run on their terms and not on the terms of those who thought they knew better. Imposition and condescension are not just bad, they can be disastrous, for they lead not just to alienation, disinterest and disenchantment, but frequently to far worse anti-community expressions.

Think about that story of the art class. There the young people were working on their own terms and although the form of the experience was imposed by their teacher, the institution provided no restraints. For the art class the barriers were by-passed to a positive and meaningful contribution. The terms they worked under were their own. The uniformed girls became part of the system; the real changes were beyond them.

We have seen that young people with a particular skill can use it for the benefit of the community. In the literacy scheme a benevolent professional provided the impetus and the opportunity to make use in this case, of the ability to read in a socially useful way. Take heart from the fact that others share his attitude and do not merely admit outsiders, but appreciate that they have much to contribute that is really needed and can change institutionalized attitudes. Such sympathetic professionals are not always found, though.

Then is the possession of a skill, however mundane, the key to the institution?

At Nottingham's Mapperley Hospital [one of the largest psychiatric centres in the country] I have been running an Origami course with two groups of about twelve patients and staff each, working each group on an alternative week so that everyone has one and a half hours instruction in a fortnight. Each session includes two, or sometimes three, models; the paper used is one foot square, and flat bone folders originally bought by the Occupational Therapy Unit for clay modelling are a great help to the class for making firm creases. The programme began with easy and attractive folds (Waterbomb, Flapping Bird, Junk) but is now structured to lay emphasis on one basic fold or procedure each time. Patients are also going to help with Christmas decorations for a local geriatric hospital.

There are two groups. One consists of admissions and short-stay patients, those who are actually resident in the hospital, permanently or temporarily. The second group is composed of medium and long-term patients – those who attend the hospital while living at home. The second group were more able to follow up their interest in Origami by practice of the models taught, and in some cases by further research from books and television; hence they have tended to enjoy it more. But nearly everyone who has participated in either group has found Origami beneficial and enjoyable. Particular types of case for which the art is successful include depressives, neurotics, alcoholics, those in the early stages of schizophrenia, and psychopathic personalities (those who have no ability to judge between right and wrong).

The occupational therapist associated with the work commented: 'Origami is an ideal group activity for all ages, stimulating interest, improving concentration and manual dexterity.' Points in favour of Origami in this field are:

1. The rapidity with which results can be achieved. This is especially important for inadequate patients who are often surprised to find that they have made something quite spectacular.

2. Mistakes are never serious and can be easily rectified, thus encouraging boldness in the handling of the paper.

3. Members of the group who have a flair for the craft can help others, thus establishing personal relationships in a natural and easy way; this is in addition to the teacher–patient relationship (remembering that the teacher in this case is someone not professionally engaged in psychotherapy).

4. Accurate and neat folding is called for, and is encouraged in those

whose condition or disposition might lead them to slovenly folding, by the example of the teacher, and, more important, by competition with other members of the group.

5. Judgement in the handling of paper is frequently needed in those models which are representations of real life. In folding a dog, for example, the patient must judge for himself how far back to slant the neck, how large to make the head, where to put the ears, etc. This type of manoeuvre appears to sharpen the faculties and stimulate the creative imagination. (Hence some patients will exclaim that their model will be a boxer, or a sausage dog.)

Perhaps the underlying reason for the success of Origami as psychotherapy is that it offers a world that the patient can control: the paper will lay flat where he decides to put it, and is subject entirely to his will. In addition, Origami offers relaxation and absorption in an easily attainable but quite profound way.[33]

The author of this piece is Paul Castles, from the sixth form at Nottingham High School.

Paul possesses a skill which enables interaction to occur – his skill brings the outside world into this mental hospital and makes it a little less of a mental hospital. Does this make our outsiders secret agents who, having gained access through their skill-attributes turn around and send the professionals packing? Will there be sit-ins comparable with student demonstrations? Hardly. Once there is a pattern of participation the institution ceases to be exclusive and belongs to the community. Community care becomes a reality. The right to care will derive from willingness rather than qualification.

Skills are required for participation, then, whether in art or Origami. Isn't this just an extension of the rules of entry? Certainly not. We all have skills which are necessary. Some people really do have the ability to sit and converse (a skill often attributed to every young volunteer, who is expected to *love* visiting the elderly). Some can make a fair job of hairdressing; some claim expertise in washing-up; others prefer TV and a laugh. All of these are skills, and skills with social value. We tend to undervalue them at present. It is particularly important that those who are learning and developing skills can practise them where they wish. Our institutions are resources for learning, with a place for everybody. By becoming aware of this (the benevolent professional) or by being made aware of it (the entry of the skilled outsider), they become more than educational resources, they become absorbed into the community.

We sometimes begin our talks on community service by asking how many of the audience shave. 'What's he on about?' Well, shaving is another skill that often needs a little developing among this age group. Boys at school in the Midlands developed it by stopping for half an hour at the male geriatric ward in the local hospital on the way to school and each shaving one man. Girls were not excluded from this learning process; on the way home the female patients were welcoming guinea pigs for rinses, shampoos and sets!

Elsewhere, young people were up to other things. Radio Northwick Park didn't hit the headlines when it began, but then this was no ordinary pirate station:

> The music fades up and Paul closes the mike for an aside to fellow programme announcer Phil Wilson: 'I've got a professional engagement for us, man, this disco at...'
>
> Upstairs, in the great concrete and glass city that is the new Northwick Park Hospital, Mrs Kathleen Day, like hundreds of other patients, was enjoying the show over her bedside head-set. She nearly dropped the cup of tea the nurse was handing her when told that slick disc-jockey Paul was still at school.... 'They're so professional,' she said.
>
> The forty or more youngsters who run Radio Northwick Park, would have it that way. Their aim is to provide a complete local radio service linking the hospital with its outside community and connecting the many units within the building itself.[34]

Not just record requests, either. You might meet someone from Radio Northwick Park interviewing in the street, recording material that will prevent patients getting that 'cut-off' feeling by keeping them in touch with local affairs. There is interviewing in the wards, too – collecting record requests and keeping in contact with patients who don't have visitors. It's a way to let people know what is going on in the hospital: why the central heating has broken down, how long until it will be mended. The things which seem frustrating when days are too long.

One thing leads to another. In Worksop boys were visiting old people in hospital. Conversations revealed that it was hard for many of these patients to see the Christmas cards on their bed-side lockers, since it required an awkward turn to do so. The boys designed and made two dozen collapsible frames at school. These slipped onto the bed and cards could be pinned onto them. Similarly a school in North Wales produced outsize chessmen and boards, finger exercisers and the answers to many of their local hospital design needs.

'What can these young volunteers do in this children's home that my staff can't accomplish?'

'They can climb trees.'

3 Community 1

It is hard, of course, to be clear about what represents an institution and what does not. In the preceding chapter we made no attempt to define exactly what we meant by 'an institution'. It is easy to recognize the school, the hospital, the old folks' home, the prison, the psychiatric hospital, the childrens' home, the approved school and the Cheshire home as institutions, because they occupy buildings. But other institutions are not recognizable in such a physical way: probation services, social services, youth services, are all fields which have become institutionalized. By this we mean that they have developed the characteristics of the building-type institution, the rules, the jargon, the so-called 'professionalism' and all the rest of it. But the activities of these bodies are not confined to the probation *office*, the social services *department* and the youth *club*. Their fields spread out into the community, though, as we have already seen, each institutionalized area of activity has peculiarly little to do with the others. They are, in the broadest sense, 'community services'.

There are institutions on a higher plane, though we have little concern with them here except to point out that schools, hospitals, universities, police stations and prisons, while institutions in themselves, are local representations of the institutionalized fields of education, health, higher education and, for lack of better words, crime and punishment.

For the moment let us just say that many aspects of our lives have become institutionalized in this way, and so time and again the community is faced with a group of professionals who have carved out niches for themselves to operate. Before embarking on a discussion of what communities are and what chance the 'willing' individual has within them, let us acknowledge that much of what we said in the previous chapter about *physical* institutions applies equally to institutionalized 'fields of work'. On that note of unbridled pessimism, let us begin.

There is always some bright spark, thank goodness, in an audience at a school, who will ask us exactly how we define this 'community' that we talk about. Clearly someone could write a book about it. As an ideal it has always been discussed and dreamed of, but as yet not found, which lets us off the hook a little. There are religious communities, as we can see in Ulster and Bangladesh. But these are communities in the simplest sense, a group of people sharing one thing in common. One regards sceptically the declaration 'Our school is a community in itself', for while the inmates have school in common, making the statement superficially true, there is little, as we shall see later, of the interaction which seems to us to mean real community. For the same reason a church might regard its congregation as a community because the members are all together on Sunday, and a town might call itself a community, defining the boundaries of community around those who shop there, and pay their rates there and use the library, and so on. But such communities are hardly more than names on a list and are not recognized as communities by the people who form them.

A community, a real vibrant living community, is a group of people, few or many, who genuinely interact with one another. Interact? That sounds suspiciously like jargon. A community is a group of people who do not delegate, or allow to be delegated, functions and services which affect them. A community is a group of people who help and service one another. A group of people who can balance the desire for privacy with a thought for the loneliness of the spinster next door. A group of people who cooperate. It is our belief that such a group needs to recognize some kind of nodal point, somewhere that they can take both their need and their willingness, a real community 'centre'. We believe that such a point could be a school, though a school very different from the sort we know at present. First we must examine the qualities, if there are any, of 'community life', by looking back, and by looking around.

At other times in the past, and in other places at present, there were and are communities in which the functions of education, welfare, even industry, to name but three, did not or do not exist in the present established senses of the words. For in these communities people taught one another, they didn't delegate the function of education to the school; people looked after one another and social services departments were not needed; people grew their own food and manufactured their own goods on an individual or cooperative basis. With the increasing specialization of the food and manufacturing industries fostered dramatically by the industrial revolution, we lost sight of our cooperative heritage. Dazzled by the ease and economy of getting others to grow food for us while we manufactured goods for them, we somehow managed to allow the same principles of ease and economy to take over the other fields. And so developed the professionalized functions not only of industry, but of education and welfare. To keep the perspective as wide as possible, here are a few of the other functions: the maintenance of law and order; the punishment of offenders; the provision of roads; the building of houses; defence; health; even such ridiculous things as hair-cutting and shoe-polishing. While we can still choose, at the moment, to delegate these latter functions, we have mentioned them because a possibility looms that before long we shall have forgotten how to perform the business ourselves – just as we have lost the confidence and ability to educate our offspring, look after our elders and the less fortunate, and even grow our own food.

Then an amazing change is upon us! Having cheerfully delegated the function of food provision we now begin to be alarmed at how badly 'they' are doing it for us. They are using additives which harm us and containers which we cannot destroy. Perhaps we should halve our lawn space and grow a few lettuces and carrots for ourselves? And besides this, what of the spiralling prices which appear in spite of subsidies which originate from our own pocket? So we start fighting to regain what we gave away.

Having cheerfully delegated the function of education to schools and teachers, we find that they are not producing the goods. Oh yes – they produce fine winners who sail away to further promote the present systems, generally as part of the hierarchy in some institution or other. But what awful, badly equipped losers! Schools are falling down on the job we gave them to do.[35] But the previous chapter has shown the reader that it is a far more difficult proposition here to regain what is rightfully ours. It is easy and legal enough to grow your own food and 'do-it-yourself' instead of purchasing manufactured items, but just try *not* sending your children to school. It isn't easy and in most cases it's illegal. Or try setting up an alternative to the present school system, but be wise enough to read about the difficulties of the Liverpool Free School first.

On now to the caring industry. The admiration of ease and economy has led us to delegate someone else to do our caring for us. After all, time spent looking after a sick, elderly or handicapped relative or friend is time spent away from our work, and the sum total of all the work is the gross national product, and if the GNP is low, then watch out, because that means your country is 'underdeveloped'! Of course, 'underdeveloped' is an economic word. Often, however, its connotations rub off on the social structure and conduct of the people. Underdeveloped means that many children do not attend school to learn the lingua franca of that particular country; that there are not many hospitals and never any old folks' homes. Underdeveloped countries may have street Koran schools where little boys learn much profundity and Arabic to boot, but Arabic is unacceptable as a sign of development and native doctors quite out of the question. It is almost a cliché to point out that in the 'underdeveloped' world the young aren't sent out in posses on certain afternoons which suit the timetable to cheer up the old folk. Elders live with you naturally; you respect them, naturally. The very name, 'elder', carries with it a dignity missing from our 'pensioner' with its economic undertones, or our 'old people', 'senior citizen'. Under developed countries are short on children's homes too. In general extended family systems, and the high value that people who have little place on little children, takes care of the parentless. Here is an exception to demonstrate the above rule. Joe was a pupil in a school in West Africa in which we worked. He came to us when he was thrown out of school for failing to produce his £20 per term school fees. His parents had both been killed in a lorry accident. Normally, responsibility for his schooling would have been assumed by his uncle, who would care for him as his own child. Joe's uncle was a rich man and there was nothing to prevent him taking the responsibility for Joe. But uncle had completed his education in Europe, and there he had observed that a man cares for his own sons and after that for himself, so he became rich in buildings and cars, and Joe became what will surely be an increasing side-effect of development – unwanted. Poor old Joe. A more typical example of the extended family system is Isaac. Isaac's brother, who was a primary school teacher and a young man, paid Isaac's £20 per term, which meant most of his own pay packet. As the cause of ease and economy gains in such countries, are we going to see more Joes and less Isaacs? It seems certain.

So here we are beginning to arrive at something: a community which does not delegate every conceivable function, which maybe accepts the logicality of having certain functions of food and manufacture performed by groups within the community or outside, but does not deceive itself into thinking that it is better to delegate functions which can be fulfilled by simple human interaction. These functions go beyond the examples of education and welfare which we have used to illustrate our point, though they are the most obvious areas on which to start. It is interesting to note that as the cause of ease and economy makes more and more of us unemployed, or working shorter working weeks, or having longer holidays, there does now seem to be an opportunity for many members of society to start retrieving some of those delegated functions in the social sector. This in turn could start a chain reaction by releasing onto the unemployment queue people like teachers, social workers, policemen, probation officers, planning officers, nurses, psychiatrists, who have professional functions in the social sector. In short, the community will exist when it takes over its own 'community services'.

Communities of cooperating individuals are getting harder and harder to find. The African village, with elements of community life in it, will disappear, as Goldsmith's Auburn disappeared, and for all Goldsmith's sentiment and nostalgia, these places have something to show us about living together. There is a struggle ahead, for the social units which existed prior to the industrial revolution do not exist now. Conurbia and suburbia, those economic units, have replaced them. Sterile high-rise flats and new estates stand where communities once thrived, and six-lane highways can divide as effectively as any Berlin Wall. And of course, people often live far from where they work, making dormitories out of places that should be playgrounds. In between the houses the paraphernalia of our economic life, the shopping centres and the factories, are dead at weekends and in the evenings. When they are open they are designed to avoid contact between persons as much as possible. Rows of shelves, wire baskets and cashiers, the persistent drone of machinery. Hardly a warm environment for meeting and enjoying one another, and consequently we do it less and less. Clearly these are not providing a focal point for the community – so we return to the school once more.

Perhaps the saddest facet of present-day communities, or rather, the places where we live, is that we simply do not feel a part of them. We do not regard these places as something which belong to us at all. More specifically, *things* don't belong to us. Talk to most people about vandalism and they will express their horror at the irresponsibility of young people: 'Just look at them – they've got more money, more free time, more outlets than I ever had at their age, and all they do is go around smashing up phone boxes, wrecking toilets and daubing walls.'

They do, too. Especially in those urban areas of high-rise and concrete we have described. You can see it everywhere. But why? Do we really provide enough outlets for youthful exuberance and enough opportunities for excitement? Are more youth clubs, football pitches and adventure playgrounds needed? Shouldn't they be provided? Provided, provided . . . more and more of the same, provided by the authorities for use by us, with the celestial knowledge possessed by all authorities of what we need. Without any reference to us. And the more facilities that are provided, the more professionals must appear to staff and support them. More youth clubs, football pitches and adventure playgrounds are not the answer, though that does not imply that the Youth Service is doing a splendid job already. It is not, and it fails in the way that other delegated caring functions are failing. Kids are still bored, aggressive and more nervous and insecure than they should be. Not all kids but enough to have made a strong impression on us. Why?

We mentioned in the last chapter that we thought the young people of Easterhouse wrecked their club in 1970 because the club, although *for* them, was not *by* them. In a television programme about the closure of the club, the city authorities were shocked by the ingratitude of the club destroyers. 'After all we did for you' echoed through their comments. A dangerous position to take, as any parent knows who has taken it once and seen the growing aggression in their child. If any attitude is guaranteed to aggravate more than another it is the expectation of gratitude. We recognize it in the family, but has the similarity with their own attitude ever struck a providing council? The phone boxes and toilets and walls in our environment are there by courtesy of some authority. They are for us, but they are not ours. The phone boxes belong to the GPO, not to us; the toilets belong to the local council, not to us; and the walls are part of the tube station or somewhere, not our walls.

Is it only young people who vandalize? In violent, physical ways, it tends to be. But watch the commuters casting their dog ends on the platform and the track; watch the 'let's have a drive this Sunday' brigade strewing the country with litter and fouling the air with noise and fumes. The stations and country are for them, but they don't belong to them. The vandalism of the older generation is more polite, but just as destructive, and it is symptomatic of the same root cause. For while a concerted intellectual effort on the part of the individual may reveal that they *are* his phone boxes because he has paid his bill and income tax, that they *are* his toilets because he has paid his rates, and it is his tube because he has paid his fare, yet it is rather hard to *feel* this responsibility, it is so obscured for most people. But if we can begin to regard these things as *by* us, as well as for us, then we are getting nearer to this idea of 'interaction' which we used to describe the working of a community. *By* means interaction, *for* means provision.

If vandalism in its violent forms is characteristic of young people, then apathy is an equally debilitating disease among the older population. We can blame everything on 'them', and of course 'they' are the professionals we have delegated to take care of 'it'. But we don't see 'their' mistakes and inadequacies as our fault. For 'they' are often no longer responsible to us, so we think.

'They put up the rates without warning us.'
'They don't provide enough playgroups.'
'They seem to spend more on maintaining the footpaths than on looking after the roads.'
'One day there was a beautiful building there, and the next day it was gone – they pulled it down for a new supermarket.'
'They really should be doing more for the old people.'

Here it is not so much that things don't belong to us, but rather that professionals – 'they' – don't seem to be responsible to us, though theoretically they are supposed to work for us.

There may be several reasons for their not being responsible to us and indeed, on occasion, appearing to act against our interests. Firstly, we may never bother to offer them much in the way of *opinion*. That is, if 'they' do implement some ghastly policy, did we tell them that we were against it? This raises the second reason: we never told them, because they never told us. It goes without saying that it is generally for reasons of ease and economy that 'they' never told us: 'After all, it is hardly reasonable to expect us to circulate every household asking for an opinion on a local issue, for there would be all shades of opinion forthcoming from a few, while the majority wouldn't bother to reply.' Thirdly 'they' have developed institutionalized barriers to public participation which we have mentioned before: jargon, promotion of the idea that they know best, and if possible, an office or department to deter the outsider from making his presence or opinion felt. Fourthly 'they' do develop an expertise which they deny to us, and it is naturally against their interests to let us in on this. So it came to pass that a large portion of the colour magazine of a Sunday newspaper was, last year, devoted to telling us the do's and don'ts of how to go about opposing or exposing 'them' and their decision. Useful, but alarming – beating 'them', but on their terms.

Conveniently, therefore, we can blame them for our own apathy. We cannot do anything, indeed we can't even *think* of doing anything, because we know, or think we know, that it will never be any use. And of course, such solutions as not paying rates will simply land us in jail. For the law is on their side, not ours. The laws are on the side of ease and economy, not individual and community decision.

These two symptoms which we have picked on, vandalism and apathy, would never have arisen, had we maintained certain social norms. On the broadest front, for example, children should be brought up in a society to which they belong and which belongs to them. Then, we might well find that they did not offend it by vandalizing and not caring about it. But our children do not have this background and consequently they do not care much about the things and people and nature that make up their environment. It is some alien place in which they find themselves rather than any habitat in the true sense of the word. 'They', on our behalf, have given us laws to take the place of lost norms. If vandalism, the physical and pointless destruction of property, is criminal, so surely is the vandalism of those despoilers of the country who construct motorways and knock down trees. That's how it looks to many kids, anyway. And they find that not only they, but everybody, is considered incapable of setting up and observing norms of behaviour without some legal sanction. Norms like 'Please don't drop litter' and 'Please leave this shelter as you would expect to find it' are replaced by warnings: 'Litter: £5 Fine' 'Maximum fine for the first offence: £100'. Legal sanctions with a little economic coercion. People should, if they think about one another at all, regard it as an acceptable norm not to allow their dogs to annoy other people. A notice on the local recreation ground issues a stern warning to the same effect signed 'By order of the council'. So once again a small area of personal negotiation is taken over by officialdom, and presumably those suffering annoyance from a dog stride off to the council offices and lodge their complaint, instead of sorting the whole thing out with the dog owner. Or frantically gesticulating at the notice they draw attention to their 'rights'. Somehow our very dignity is handed over for administration by authorities. Replacing norms by laws is symptomatic of their control and our apathy, which has both led to and been fostered by it.

Then the law can effectively prevent our participating in or influencing community life. Take, for example, the group of young mothers who want to form a playgroup. The council must approve their premises before they can embark upon this kind of basic communal venture. The whole rigmarole seems designed to make sure that no project will ever get off the ground. Forms are filled in and formal requests made, and if 'they' say no then you break the law if you begin. Surely parents and children themselves should have some say in the type of education they will have, yet look at the difficulties faced by potential free schools. Why can we not say what we want, complain if our school fails us? But we are faced with councils, inspectors, the law. By our choice, our participation, our initiative and our norms we should be in a position to decide what we want, how we want to do it, and then be able to do it. At the moment we don't, or perhaps we can't – or can we?

This picture we have painted of the way the community has delegated functions, particularly of 'community services', to professionals, does not represent the whole situation. For, over the years, gaps have been perceived in these services, where nobody in particular seems to be doing a job that needs doing. Various groups of people have sprung up to cater for needs which are not fulfilled by 'them'. Sadly, what tends to happen is that these very groups of philanthropic people become institutions in themselves. Yes, it is sad, but it has happened. The amateurs are sucked into the professional hose and come out as 'voluntary services' to supplement the institutional 'statutory services' we have talked of. The very names are off-putting, with that dry-as-dust tone of the bureaucrat and administrator which is guaranteed to destroy willing. The Youth Service itself illustrates this process. Originally, it seems, it came into being because the 'uniformed' services for youth were not attractive to all young people, smacking, perhaps, rather too much of the 'organization'. Not all young people wanted to spend their spare time in the Boy Scouts, the Boys' Brigade or the Guides. So the concept of the youth club was born: non-uniformed with informal activities. That was fine, but paradoxically, from community-orientated origins, the Youth Service (note those capitals, sure label of an institution) has become even more divorced from community control than the uniformed services. Only the part-time youth leaders, local people who want to help, really represent the community aspect of the youth service, and they are the ones who are made to feel inadequate in a now highly professionalized field of work.

Or, to take another example, look at Meals on Wheels. A need was spotted. Old people needed cheap, nourishing meals supplied to them. A group of philanthropic and thoughtful people responded to this need. Generally they were people with *time* – middle-aged women. But they now control the function, and like all good institutionalized fields of work, by catering for the need, they encourage apathy among the community as a whole. Surely there is someone down the road, or even next door, who could cook for two, instead of one? Surely there is, but because 'they' deliver the meals, our apathy, our lack of thought and interest, is encouraged. Here again, voluntary beginnings have led to statutory conclusions, and this particular field is just as closed to the outsider as if the service were run from the statutory social services department, as it now often is, in many areas.

And don't think that because organizations deal with larger areas and more people, that they will necessarily do things better than the neighbour who takes in a plate of stew to the old lady next door. Have you ever had an institution meal?

If all this gives the impression that we are damning the voluntary services that exist, then it is wrong. The very existence of voluntary services, their very beginnings, show that people do want to give service to others. That is fine and laudable, and the organizations which began from such willingness are laudable too. But once they become exclusive, as they have often done, and have 'rules' of entry and a 'professionalism' which puts off the ordinary person, then, far from being a service, they are performing a disservice, for willingness must be the only criterion for a person to serve, not age or accent or background or old-style philanthropic motives.

This tendency for what began as a voluntary service to become statutory, is alarming and counter-productive, for it encourages the same kind of apathy, ignorance and passivity as institutions create. What a pity it is that something that was originally by the community and for the community like Meals on Wheels, has become simply 'for it' and by a group of 'professional' volunteers. In view of this it is even more urgent that the statutory should become voluntary, or more correctly, that we should have community services by the community, for the community. The services will be less efficient, but more personalized and far more friendly.

And, more important still, action which begins with the community now must stay with the community. Talk about locating a need, catering for it and then 'handing it over to the statutory department' worries us. Yet this often happens. We remember hearing from a teacher of design and technical studies, who described to us how some of his boys had themselves designed a ramp which enabled a wheelchair user to get in and out of his house in ease and safety. This was a far better piece of equipment than the knock-up piece of carpentry the disabled man had been using before. Marvellous, we thought. A good example of the community – here a group of school boys – taking over a responsibility. Were more to be designed and built for other handicapped people in the town, we asked? The answer was no, for such ramps were manufactured, to the boys' design, by the Bath Institute of Medical Engineering in some far away place. A fine job was done, but then handed over to 'them'. So the young people, instead of being encouraged to take on a responsibility of which they were capable, were merely shown that there is somebody else organized to do the job with more ease and economy than they could manage and they might as well forget about ramps for the disabled, because that is all taken care of now. This excellent scheme thus failed to make the vital educational point that to take a responsibility is better than to pass it on.

Here we will put the philosophy behind us for a while and look at this whole community business rather more practically. Let us look at three recent Acts of Parliament, all of which should long ago have been accepted as norms, but, for reasons we have shown, have become laws. These offer scope for a takeover bid by the community, though, as so often happens, these Acts delegate the functions concerned to local government.

The 1970 Chronically Sick and Disabled Persons Act – see how the title is something official, nothing to do with 'me' – required local authority social services departments to locate handicapped people in their area and cater for their needs. A formidable task and one for which, by and large, the departments concerned will admit that they are hopelessly ill-equipped. Remember, the department will tell you, it is dealing with an enormous load of family casework, individual casework and residential care. For ventures of this sort, locating the handicapped (putting aside their needs, for the moment!), they are simply understaffed. The result is, of course, that they cannot do it, though in this case it is doubtful whether we will criticize them since it does not concern us. But it *does* concern us.

Outset, a small charity trying to raise funds for quite a different purpose, the single homeless, was the first to offer a solution to the problem. Outset got young people to raise money for them by sponsored community work, and they thought: 'Why don't kids deliver leaflets to every household in a social services department area?' The leaflets say, to put it simply, that if you are handicapped or if you think that you are entitled to any of these benefits – free telephone, free home help, etc. – then return the attached business reply card. Outset naturally saw that the departments concerned could print the leaflets, as financial resources are not the problem here, and the children from local schools could deliver them on a sponsored basis.

So we are saying that local social services departments should use child labour to do their work for them, are we? In a way, yes, though that needs clarifying. What we are saying, or rather, what we *do* say to young people is 'Go to your local director of social services and suggest he takes it easy over the Alf Morris Act. (Alf Morris was the MP who sponsored the 1970 Act). Tell him: we, the young people of this area, will locate the handicapped. If he has any sense at all he'll fall over himself trying to help you. He will print the leaflets and provide the materials you need, particularly if you point out to him that your way is the best chance of a successful survey, since kids at school do live in just about every street in the area. Deliver the leaflets, but the reply cards are not sent back to the 'department'. They're sent back to you at the school. So you start to cater for the needs of the handicapped, not them. The handicapped are your responsibility, aren't they?

It takes a little longer to describe the idea than that, and as a scheme it cannot work ideally in some ways at the present time.

But basically it means that young people, when they know where the handicapped are in their area, actually cater for the needs of the handicapped, rather than leaving it to the professional department. Do not believe for a moment that the professionals will do this better. For a start, there will be so many new 'clients' that they will respond to needs only slowly, and, very probably, inadequately. So not only can we do it, but we can do it better, and the handicapped are now our responsibility, not theirs. So far, so good, but where do we go from there? The school must now serve the community's interests. At the moment the school is not the way we should like to see it. It is still basically a place for young people only. Later we explain how we see it in the future as a place for *all* people. However, at present, we cannot cater completely for all the needs of the local disabled from the schools, for not all the necessary skills will be found there. If there were more to the school than young people being educated in the current fashion, then more would be possible right now. But there is no need to be deterred because the system is this way at the moment. Read on.

The people determine the needs. The young people determine the needs. A ramp needed? – We make it in school. Doors need widening? Handrails fitting? – We can do that. But what about that free telephone? What about providing day and night attendance? Perhaps it is here that we would be reluctantly forced to say: inform the department. But hold on – can't *we* tell the GPO? Can't we arrange, even from amongst our own ranks, our own relatives, our own acquaintances, for help with that constant attendance? One begins to see that if the school were the focal point of community life, and society adjusted to that fact, then problems could be solved without reference elsewhere. This would mean that the handicapped would naturally become part of the school's life in a reciprocal way. They'd be in the mainstream, not forgotten people relying on services from the state and the local department.

The handicapped don't need services only in their own homes. What about the local area? Does it cater for their needs? Can wheelchairs get into the library, the swimming pool, the school, local shops, toilets and cinemas?

'Well, there aren't many handicapped people around here, you see, so all this talk about catering for them is irrelevant.'

'How do you know?'

'You never see any of them, do you?'

That's exactly the point. We don't see all that many handicapped people around because we institutionalize many of them. And those who do live in the community are limited in their ventures when every kerb is as good as a cliff and every flight of stairs a mountain range.

The school surveys the area. It carries out what has come to be called a 'wheelchair survey':

During the first few months after Christmas the task of surveying the city of Swansea was carried out by eighty girls. The whole of Swansea was sub-divided into districts and, in some cases, into streets, and teams of girls were assigned to cover the various sections of the town...

It became apparent before long that while the suburbs were adequately covered, the centre of the city was not. Thus a second, supplementary survey of the centre of the town was conducted. Sixth-form girls were given permission by the local education authority and by their headmistress to use their free time during school hours to undertake this supplementary survey...

The girls were able to work quickly and easily in the familiar, personal and friendlier atmosphere of the smaller surburban shops while the impersonal atmosphere of the city centre demanded more forceful and resolute personalities...[36]

Such surveys can result in the publication of handbooks for the disabled in a particular area. These books note the location of the shops, cinemas, toilets etc., which *are* suitable for the disabled and are naturally extremely useful to handicapped people. An excellent project, but more can be done. We should like to see 'surveyors' then concentrating on those establishments which don't appear in the book. What about the school, for a start? What about the local football ground? Why can't the soccer enthusiasts try getting into the ground in a wheelchair and writing to the manager and players if they can't? The ramps can be built in the school. If the library or 'disco' offer shortage of cash as the excuse, perhaps with money provided by the social services department. Indeed, the function of 'them', the department, will be reduced to just that. The community will do the rest. Initiatives will come from young people in school. Or will exams always be the priority in schools?

Let us look now at country amenities for a moment. The Countryside Act of 1968 delegated, as before, the responsibility for maintaining ordinary public footpaths to local councils. One is impressed by the bold 'Public Footpath to. . . .' signs that one sees when driving down country lanes.

Suddenly, a sprouting of public footpath signs is forcing itself on the attention of travellers in many parts of the country. The Countryside Act, 1968, which gives local authorities the duty of erecting signs, sometimes on private land as well as public highways, is taking positive effect.[37]

Great. So 'they' are up to scratch in this respect, are they? Well, no, very often it seems they are not. As before one cannot exactly say it is 'their' fault. Rather, once again, it is beyond 'their' means. The signs do look very impressive, it is true. But just try actually walking along one of the paths. Far too often once you get beyond the entry point at the road you find yourself no longer on a public footpath but in the middle of a public blackberry bush. Or the way is barred by a fence put there by a local farmer or a local industry.

I have tried to follow footpath routes, near Gawsworth, Cheshire, and several miles away in the Nether Alderley area; but in one case there was no apparent continuation, and in the other crops effectively prevented the use of a way beside a fence.

Taking the right way would be a matter of luck in many cases, for there was no other sign. Now, however, some local authorities are using waymarks so that the walker knows where he can go and there is no needless trespass.[38]

You see, 'they' cannot deal with it all. Try ringing your local council and asking how many people are employed in the highways and planning departments. Then get out your local Ordnance Survey map and measure how many miles of highways, lanes, sidewalks and footpaths there are. Now divide the number of miles of roads and paths by the number of 'them'. A tough job for 'them' isn't, it?

What, therefore, can be done about the obstructive blackberry bushes and fences? Obviously you will not get anywhere by simply writing to complain, either to the council, or the local paper, though it might be worth trying the farmer or industrialist concerned. There are occasional results from this method, but here is a more reliable scheme for footpath reclamation. The paths are our responsibility, so let us begin there, and discuss again what the *school* can do.

In 1968 the Countryside Commission, a semi-institutionalized voluntary body, mounted an ambitious 'Rights of Way' survey by schools all over the country. The aim was to get children to discover the fences and blackberry bushes on public paths and where possible to take action to reclaim the path. Let us hope this didn't give the chilren the impression that it was the Countryside Commission who would then take care of the path. It seems that nobody exists to take care of the paths except the people who like them and wish to use them. And though they and the schools can get rid of that bush, and any school-based maintenance team can deal with the seats that need repairing, the stiles that need fixing, the signs that need painting and the litter bins that need locating, what about the fence? Here we can learn from the Ramblers Association, though again, we cannot sit back and think that they are looking after our responsibilities. The following quotation is from a story by a member of the Peak and Northern Footpaths Society, Donald Lee. Using the towpath of the Manchester, Bolton and Bury canal, a pleasant walk in the south Lancashire industrial belt, he found that a fence had been erected across the path by a local paper mill. According to the mill, this was to protect their property, and they had been informed by the local council that there were no rights of way across the land. Later the council had consulted their map, after complaints from the public, and asked the firm to remove the fence. The firm refused to do so and the council, probably embarrassed by their own error, indicated that they were not prepared to take legal action.

Three years of inactivity passed. In mid-1969, the Ramblers Association held a meeting to form a Bolton Group and I spoke on local issues, including the towpath affair. This got plenty of press publicity and comment, but even so Broadbents (now part of the Trinity Paper Mill

Group) refused to budge. The file was passed to our solicitors with instructions to prosecute under the Highways Act 1959 for wilful obstruction. The paper mill pleaded guilty before the Bolton Magistrates Court in October 1969. The maximum fine is £50, but the magistrates considered that the defendants had been the victims of an 'administrative muddle' and they were fined a nominal £1. However, we had achieved our objective and the footpath was reopened.[39]

Is this kind of action beyond the school? It is surely not, particularly if the school could call on the cooperation of the adults in its community. After all, most of us are faced with legal complexities some time or other, and a visit to the Old Bailey or the local magistrates court is not going to make our own problems much clearer. So, if all else fails, why shouldn't a school take an offender to court? It may be unlikely, but should the need arise, as it did in the account above, we will have taken the responsibility, a responsibility which will eventually, we hope, lead to the law becoming a norm. Again, isn't this kind of real learning important? Won't it appeal more to some young people than book-learning, and isn't it more relevant to real life? What better practical geography lesson than one which starts with a visit to the local council to see or get the definitive maps that show where paths should be? Compasses would be needed as well as tools. Fifteen-year-olds we know are highly enthusiastic about the idea.

We mentioned earlier the schools who offer 'voluntary service' as an alternative to games, the CCF and orienteering. We can think of no better way of involving them all than by suggesting that the most successful method of tramping out a footpath is by feet in rugger or army boots.

Lastly, the Caravan Sites Act (1968). This was meant to be a kind of 'Bill of Rights' for gypsies and other travellers. Again, the Act told local authorities what they should be doing, and what they had to do in this case was to provide permanent sites, with all the necessary facilities and amenities, for local travellers. The parallel with the Chronic Sick and Disabled Persons Act is clear. This time the 'location' of gypsies was done in a government survey some years before 1968[40] and the 1968 Act now required local authorities to cater for the needs of gypsies, namely, to provide sites for them. The Act was, one

assumes, not simply responding to the needs of gypsies, but to the demands of people who saw the value of their houses lowered by gypsy encampments on the roadside verges, and of the police, growing as tired as the gypsies were themselves, of enforcing laws which forbid camping on roadside verges. But where are the caravan sites? Why haven't 'they' got on with it and provided them? Why aren't 'they' helping the gypsies – or why aren't they maintaining our house values?

What has happened is that 'they' are prevaricating. Each council is waiting for neighbouring councils to move first, in the hope that their gypsies will move to the neighbouring sites and thus solve the whole problem most neatly.

In a bid to get rid of the gypsies in Dunton Green, the parish council is to ask Kent County Council to plant trees on their site while they are away fruit picking.

At last week's meeting of the council it was agreed unanimously that something must be done about the gypsies, who moved into the area in great numbers during the winter.

Mrs H. Dinnis said, 'They will be going to the Marden area for the fruit picking and that is the time to clear the site and plant the trees.'

The council agreed to send a letter to the KCC asking them to do this.

Mr D. Gomez suggested that one way of getting rid of the gypsies might be to boycott their vital needs.

Lock the gate

The chairman, Mrs Glyn Davis, said, 'When I went to church on Sunday I saw them filling up huge carts with water from the allotments tap.'

Mr W. Hollands said, 'The only way to stop that is to lock the gate and provide each allotment holder with a key. If the KCC had planted trees, when we asked them to several years ago, the problem would not have occurred.

'Nine councils in the Bromley area are trying to get the law changed so they can throw the gypsies out, into the country.'[41]

Unfortunately it is harder for 'us' to take the initiative in the way we suggested for the Alf Morris Act, as this is obviously a field of intrigue, prejudice and, as we have said, prevarication. Many people don't like gypsies; most feel sympathy for the handicapped. All too often gypsies are considered 'anti-social'; it is easier for society to rise above being 'anti-handicapped'. The gypsies are criticized, even hounded, for being filthy spoilers of the environment. An offence of which none of us are guiltless, particularly our planners and builders.

This prejudice cannot be ignored, and the 1968 Act could not overcome it or allow us to forget it by siting gypsies in convenient places. We must, therefore, try to overcome it. This is where the school comes in. How many history, social studies or English courses make any attempt to provide young people with the kind of knowledge that might lead to an understanding and more willing attitude? Here, just as with old people, a school would do well to realize that it is positively fortunate to have gypsies in the area. They are the living resource for learning about their culture. Such involvement would clearly lead to greater understanding and, more important, to the realization that we can help both them and our community.

So Jimmy, whose dad is a farmer, develops a sympathy and understanding for gypsies. He tells his father, who relies on travelling people to pick his fruit and hops each summer. Together they plan a site in a field, concreted (Jimmy's school friends raise the money) and equipped with water taps and toilets.

No chance. Pretty quickly 'they' will be on the scene talking about 'planning permission' and threatening action in the courts. But why should 'they' tell us how to be good citizens? Well, these are laws made in 'our' name that are being used, remember, to control what we do with our property and what we do for the community.

Let us imagine that a school decides to provide for the needs of local gypsies because nobody else seems to be doing much for them. They undertake a local education campaign to ensure the support of local people, tell the council to 'get on' with providing a site. The latter prevaricate so the school gets on with it – on Jimmy's dad's land. The council threaten action – what can the school do? Well remember the Act required 'them' to get on with it, so who is in the wrong? 'Badger's Mount Secondary School versus Badger's Mount Borough Council.' We can't wait to see it.

BEEFSTEAK & ANDICAP
ENTRANCE A
ENTRANCE A
GOR
AND SO
LIBRARY

CHRONIC SICK AND DISABLED PERSONS ACT 1970
Access for the disabled to all public buildings
BRARIAN
AND SO
GENT
GUM

4 Community 2

In Wallingford, Berkshire, we came across the 'Shakespeare House Barracuda Club'. From the outside it looks a rather less than ordinary youth club, but its history is extremely interesting. The buildings are dreary, and the housing estate surrounding them is as sterile as its counterparts anywhere. Two huts comprise the main club buildings, block built, single storey with corrugated asbestos roofs. They are actually old army buildings. Over a period of six months they were converted by the young people of the area into their youth club. These young people formed the 'Wallingford Task Force' (nothing to do with the London organization of the same name), and since they undertook the club job, they have carried out many similar tasks in various places. Converting the old army huts was no easy task, for they were originally divided into many tiny rooms. Walls had to be knocked down, toilets and cloakrooms installed, floors cleaned and smoothed and tiled. A bar and reception lounge were built, and one of the huts was half gutted so that it could be turned into a hall.

What is so spectacular about the Barracuda Youth Club? Well, just that, the way it was made. Not long ago, when the local mayor visited the club, he remarked that it was surprising to find no broken windows or other signs of vandalism. He was told that this club belonged to the kids who used it. They and their predecessors had 'built' it. They had raised all the money for the work themselves. The club was made by them, as well as for them. At present the Club has 150 regular members and two local purpose-built clubs can't touch it in terms of popularity and lack of malicious damage.

There seems to be a lesson in the story of the Shakespeare House Barracuda Club, and it is worth contrasting this story with that of the Easterhouse Youth Club Project in Glasgow, to which we have already referred. The point is clear, and it seems worth adding that the young people of the Wallingford club didn't strike us as being more rarefied than teenage kids anywhere. In other words, what they did is within the capabilities of any group of young people.

Clearly 'provision' is not the answer. If something is 'ours' and not 'theirs' we care about it. Unfortunately the Youth Service itself has not yet learnt this particular lesson so one might feel hesitant about applying it to the wider context of the whole community. We shall do so, though first spending a little longer on the subject of youth clubs.

There are plenty of symptoms of the malaise that is supposed to be affecting young people, and school-aged young people in particular. In Northern Ireland we see them every day, beset by the frustration of most kids, but at least finding some excitement in throwing stones and provoking troops. What else is there to do which has this precious element of excitement? Share a joint, maybe. There's always a certain titillation in feeling that the hand of the law might descend on your shoulder at any moment, and also of doing something that parents claim can be dangerous in itself. Add to this the comfort of knowing from one's own experience that there isn't too much to the sin, whether it's spraying 'Chelsea' on the bus station wall or smoking pot or skiving school. And the exhilaration of that dash to avoid Mum, or teacher, or the cop as they approach. It can't be equalled by anything at school. There's an element of danger there that adults who remember depressions and wars want to protect us from. But no excitement means boredom, as often as not, and protection means denial. A London social worker was howled down at a conference for teachers when he suggested that kids might take drugs out of boredom. Have teachers never been children themselves?

So, those who don't believe kids caught at such peccadilloes should be locked up or further repressed in some way think that what these young hooligans need is Outward Bound Courses, or better still, a chance to attempt the north face of the Eiger in winter, feet first. Give them a challenge, they say, that'll sort them out. That'll work out all this energy, give them a chance to grow up. As anyone who has grown up a bit will verify, there is a certain amount of sense in this. A challenge, and on your own to face it, that's probably what taught us all something about ourselves. And kids would enjoy such chances. But sending them out on such ambitious projects all the time is not feasible, and we must start realizing that there is excitement and adventure in our own communities, which could provide a challenge for young people if allowed to do so. Most importantly, their own community can provide young people with a responsibility for their own and other people's future. But at the moment young people have very few of the rights which would make such opportunities possible. We do repress them, however liberal minded we think we are. We think them 'too young' to be responsible, so we give them no right of responsibility. In return they seek expression in behaviour which we call anti-social, since it is against our world. We regard that behaviour as proof of our own assumptions about the need to keep young people in their place, rather than as proof that our assumptions are wrong.

Tell us: is there anything wrong in saying that the 'bosses' and 'leaders' of the youth clubs in this country should be the young people themselves? Is it so wildly absurd (for many to whom we have put this idea think so) to say 'Look, this is your youth club, so over to you'? Do we really have to 'provide' youth services in the form of purpose-built clubs run by leaders and administrators who see the young people who use the club as consumers rather than partners? If we said 'Look, this is your club, so over to you', would the result be disaster? Only if nobody came any more. Often 'disaster' is used to describe kids enjoying themselves in a way we don't understand. When we provide facilities for them, we expect them to fit into the picture we paint on our terms. The result is vandalism and disenchanted kinds. The Barracuda Club understood that.

Ideally we'd like to see the Youth and Community Service people (as they call themselves) encouraging young people to provide for their own needs and for the needs of those younger than themselves. We would like to meet the Youth Officer who, having provided that encouragement, listens to the group of kids who want a youth club and says: 'Well, let's look for a place to have a club, and then you can tell me how much you want to do what you want.'

Of course, adult help and guidance will be needed. But not adult provision. Such help is there, in the community. All the skills that you need to help build, decorate, organize and set up a project: plumbers and painters and musicians and tea-makers. But most adults think that the Youth Service is the body concerned with provision for young people, and it really isn't anything to do with them. So we don't see many of them offering their services. Those that do at the moment become 'part-time youth leaders', part of the providing establishment; those that do in the future will do so out of a conscious desire to help young people run their own affairs, as at present. But they will join the young people, not the 'Youth Service'. They will not have to train, take diplomas or go on courses. Like the kids, their willingness will be their qualification. But the willingness will come only when the community, young and old, takes back the responsibility. Unfortunately 'they', who control the institutionalized field of youth work, are not so conscious as we are of their own failings, so we must adopt the same tactics here as we suggested should be used for the penetration of the institution. In the latter take-over young people will be offering their skill as young people. They will approach the institution knowing that their particular skill is that they *are* young people; the skills of the willing adults will be, above all, their ability to regard young people as equals, and not as juniors. The whole business would be a lot easier if the Youth Service would give it a try. But they will not. They are professionals and know better than us. Meanwhile we live with their failings.

Service by young people for themselves and others can take different forms. The growth of pre-school playgroups in recent years has not gone unnoticed by some teachers on the look-out for community-service projects. Many young girls 'help' in playgroups and even, though more rarely, run their own. It is obviously important for young girls and boys to get used to dealing with young children, so helping playgroups can be very valuable.

Approaches were made first to the already established playgroups in the town, which had been established for about two years. The groups had about twenty-five three to five year olds in each and were being run by a trained leader with 'a few of the mums'. The girls discussed what help they might give and the outcome was that fourteen began to go quite regularly, one morning a week . . .

It is amazing how quickly the girls have integrated into these playgroups. The leader speaks very highly of the work they do. . . . The girls feel they have also gained a lot from this experience – they have learned the value of play and what activities and equipment a child most enjoys. They also know the way to handle the difficult or isolated child – all very useful experiences to have before they leave school and start families of their own . . .[42]

This led to the school starting their own playgroup.

The day chosen by us was Market Day, and the idea of the scheme was to offer a centre at which mothers could leave their children for up to one-and-a-half hours to enable them to shop or go out visiting.[43]

But what about insurance and the law? There are laws to prevent community-minded anybodies serving their community!

Insurance regulations and the law had to be checked. Fortunately we fell foul of neither. Insurance cover was already provided by the county council to schoolgirls involved in social service activities. The law allows child minding to take place for a period not exceeding one-and-a-half hours before inspection of premises, medical examination of the helpers, etc., become necessary.[44]

We admired this story from Meridian School in Hertfordshire, and all praise to it, and the many others who have undertaken similar schemes. The pity is that far more schools have not already started such work. However, one can see why not, for the last sentence above contains the warning. Playgroups are becoming institutionalized too. 'Inspection of premises, medical examination of the helpers. . . .' This is an excellent area for young mothers, individuals and schools to take community responsibility, yet official rules and regulations imply that this too is a professional field, supervised by experts who can manage, thank you, just like their counterparts in other institutionalized welfare functions. And a playgroup in a school – what better way of encouraging the community to 'come in'? Schools could run playgroups and youth clubs and entertainments for elders, and a wide range of other services. It sounds desirable to us. It seems possible to us. Is it because it doesn't appeal to many teachers at present that many other schools have not taken up the playgroup idea demonstrated by Meridian School? Perhaps they don't want too many outsiders coming in? After all, a good deal of the mystique of the profession and of education would be revealed to the discerning in a quick half hours' whip round any school. It would hardly enhance the status of the teacher.

Returning to the Meridian account, notice the decision to hold the playgroup on a market day. That was a good idea. Another might be a group in or near a launderette. Or one in a maternity hospital, for many forbid children to accompany father at visiting time. It seems a strange rule for a maternity hospital, but, as we have said, institutions create these little rules for themselves.

This work in playgroups is very often a sensible and realistic extension of Home Economics classes for girls. Most definitely boys can also be involved, if they wish to opt for it, but what can they do if this doesn't appeal? Undoubtedly there is great scope for boys to service the playgroups, making toys and play equipment and repairing broken things. At Golden Hillock School, Birmingham, Keith Tomkinson, who teaches art, got his fourth-year leavers to produce a mural for a playgroup. As well as providing a service for the playgroup he aimed:

> To show that all areas of knowledge can be vital to an effective practical demonstration of help; that it is possible for painting to have practical use outside the classroom.[45]

Accordingly the fourth-year leavers were given opportunities to see playgroups at work on a casual visit and community-service basis and the project was discussed.

> I found it wasn't too necessary to lead them as they were quite enthusiastic over the general idea and came up with a few good pointers towards planning and design.... It was important to lead on from this by talking to the group about the sort of things little kids prefer.... We came in the end to the agreement that the kiddies might like Humpty Dumpty better than the latest thing out of BMC or BOAC.[46]

So this mural project included an exercise in seeing the other point of view, a subject for which it is often very difficult to find teaching material. So often as teachers, we are able only to put our own point of view and try to encourage our pupils to question it. Stage two of the design of the mural required the painters to divide up and produce sections of the mural on a small scale. This prototype can be used under an epidiascope or squared out to guide the painters in the assault on the playgroup wall. For the actual painting Keith Tomkinson recommends overalls! He says:

There are many danger points of non-involvement and each group member must feel he or she is an integral part of the set up . . .[47]

So one small community got involved with another and provided a service.

Paddington School in Liverpool and Llangefni School in Anglesey found other ways in which young people could provide a service for one another. The former has built the first playmobile in the country. This is an old Liverpool Corporation bus, which the school bought and the boys and girls converted into a marvellous travelling plaything. It is parked in streets to be used by young children, manned by older children. The bus cost a lot of money to buy – £120. But the school which enabled it to be built provided both an opportunity for boys and girls to give a service and learn, at the same time, more than they could glean from £120 worth of text-books about how they can be important to other, in this case younger, people. Not that the appropriate text-book exists.

In Llangefni, an adventure playground was built for the local primary school. It didn't meet the requirements which the National Playing Fields Association lay down for the ideal adventure playground. Watch out, your adventure playgrounds are being institutionalized! But really this adventure playground was better, because it was a service by young people for other young people:

The whole thing came into focus after Mr G. Warren, HMI, visited our school. . . . His interest and vision in the scrutiny of plans for new schools left us with the challenge of designing and building an adventure playground for a local primary school that was under construction.

For some time several ideas had been toyed with for developing our handicraft curriculum, but no detailed plans had been formulated. This one, though, had scope! The subject had appeal for our pupils – visions of young Tarzans flying around, etc., etc. Added to this, the very thought that they were considered to be mature enough to provide a real playground for the 'children' of the primary school, sold the idea, anyway![48]

There's a role for an inspector and a teacher, the people who enable young people to do things, and learn by doing them and provide a service for others by doing them. Mr Warren, the HMI, and Mr Thomas, the teacher and author of this article about the playground, were *enablers*, and that is a fine thing to be even if it doesn't ever achieve the status of a profession. And let us hope that in the school there will be adults who have skills in brick-laying, bus-driving or whatever, who feel that they can help, teach, learn and serve as well. Here Llangefni School showed just how to involve others, both in and out of the school.

The children were asked to devise apparatus and equipment that would be suitable. The boys did this while the girls, directed by the biology master, Mr J. Bentlet, investigated the playing habits of infants. The types of games they played; the size of the groups; the amount of space used and so on. All this was observed and noted. Infant children and their teachers were interviewed in an attempt to get as much information as possible. At this stage other factors such as safety, cleanliness ... and freedom from interference from others emerged as valid considerations. Mr Evans (art) and Mr Ward (craft) were additional consultants on design details.

Many more letters were written, shops and merchants' yards visited, telephone calls made and knowledgeable parents 'pumped'.

The need for a concrete mixer was obvious. A remarkably active and generous branch of the Round Table heard of our need and determined they could and would help. Presto! – one mixer.

A 'barrowmix' was given most readily by a local newsagent, a load of sand came from another local man. The community was not only aware of our work, it was interested and helpful.[49]

There were other teachers involved and other people in the local community. What they achieved should be heeded elsewhere. In East Kentish Town, London, for example, where 81 per cent of 400 respondents in a survey 'thought that more children's play areas were very badly needed or desirable'. Where is the school in Kentish Town which will take the initiative?

These are not the only things young people can do for one another. We shall talk about other schemes in another chapter, but here is a brief run-down to whet the appetite. Secondary schools are served by numbers of 'feeder' primary schools. Young people from the secondary schools have plenty to contribute in the primary sector, helping younger kids with everything from reading to French and football. In some places schemes enabling this interaction between young people and younger people already exist. They are often called tutoring schemes and they really do work, giving benefit to both the secondary 'tutors' and the primary 'tutees'. Why do they not occur more widely? The schemes happen where the teachers, both primary and secondary, are prepared to step down a little from their professional perch and 'admit' unqualified young people into the teaching role. Teachers are professionals and schools are their institutions, so there haven't been too many of these tutoring schemes so far.

We have talked to tutors from Haverstock School and the Central Foundation Grammar Schools for Boys and Girls, in London. Their enthusiasm for the work, their *willingness*, above all, was apparent. It was pretty abundant in the teachers who enabled the tutoring schemes to come about, too. If only a few more would be similarly 'unprofessional' in their attitude and ignore the pronouncements of the National Union of Teachers about 'unqualified' teachers, which aren't very helpful for tutoring schemes. To put it simply, many children wouldn't get behind with their reading, their maths, if they were *individually* helped, by tutors, who could be housewives, bricklayers, older children, *anyone*. And how many unsung Georgie Bests might be revealed by a bit of individual coaching? (See Chapter 7 for a discussion of tutoring in more detail.)

Young people are often ingenious and inventive. Just look at the games they think up, the 'things they manage to get up to', if you need convincing. Such ingenuity can have useful outlets, if the opportunities are provided and the encouragement given. Remember Denise Weller, and Pauline Jones, the girl who took the baby from her pram outside a supermarket? Both could have been spared their respective fates. A school in Manchester, Walkden County Secondary School, had considered just this problem many years earlier. Girls at the school invented a device, a simple circuit, that would sound an alarm bell when the removal of the baby caused the electrical circuit to become complete. Couldn't any school develop and market such a device for sale in the local area? Wouldn't the experiment bring Ohm's law, electromagnetic induction and the theory of the dry cell to real life?

Let us look at two other examples. At Brierley Street Secondary Modern School, Crewe, it was the fourth-year leavers who worked on the project; at George Watson's College, Edinburgh, the sixth-year science students. Both groups cooperated with the medical profession on solutions to two very different problems.

Dr Evan Lloyd, of the Royal Infirmary, Edinburgh, approached the sixth form at George Watson's College with a request for help. He wanted to develop a means of internally rewarming patients suffering from hypothermia (which is the term used to describe a lowering of the body's inner temperature). This was around the time that six children had tragically died of exposure in the Cairngorms, so the problem was of striking relevance. Three of the sixth formers, Messrs Conliffe, Orgel and Walker, set about tackling the problem in a most methodical manner. They, their chemistry teacher, Mr Thomson, and Dr Lloyd quickly decided that the best method of internal rewarming would be to make use of the chemical reaction between carbon dioxide, which we exhale, and soda lime, a common and simple chemical substance. This reaction is exothermic, i.e. it produces heat. So, very simply, if the carbon dioxide the patient breathes out passes through soda lime, it gets hot. If it is mixed with oxygen and then inhaled, warm air thus reaches the lungs and heart, where the warmth is most effective.

That makes it all sound very easy, but tests had to be carried out, and the design of the apparatus itself was of critical importance, for it had to be light and simple to operate, and indeed be capable of operating in extreme weather conditions. The sixth formers did it, though, and proved what young people in the academic rat-race are capable of doing, for they provided not only a useful piece of life-saving apparatus, but also a relevant edge to their education. We should remember both.

Though not so much a matter of life and death, what the fourth-year leavers did in Brierley Street School also illustrates the above principles – the school is capable of providing a service *for* the community and by doing just that it can begin to achieve some relevance in the curriculum. We should be quite clear about the kind of boys who were involved in this particular project. Their headmaster, Mr Mills, writes:

Considering the names of the boys involved, I realized that a number of the boys had appeared before different juvenile courts recently. Two of them, for instance, had been involved in smashing a sports-shop window and making off with whatever they could grab. They had no use for the articles they took but threw them away. Three others had stolen sheath knives during the school holidays and used them to threaten girls. Serious charges had been made, but the boys had claimed it was 'just a giggle'. Six others had been in trouble with the police over fighting at a Fourth Division football match. At least half [of the boys involved] had been involved in acts of hooliganism about the town and I had written reports on them for juvenile courts....[50]

The project was actually put to the boys by Alan Pemberton, a senior research fellow of the Schools Council Design and Craft Project. He asked the boys if they could design equipment which would enable children suffering from spina bifida to move around. These children were unable to walk or even use their legs, which were sometimes encased in plaster.

This project would entail considerable homework. Limbs of young children would have to be measured and their contours moulded in plaster. Sketches would have to be made, and prototypes knocked up. This might not all be done in school hours. A method of mass-production would have to be thought out. Would the lads work 'factory hours' at least from 8.30 a.m. to 5.30 p.m. on two consecutive days? Would they put in overtime if necessary, to complete the work unpaid?[51]

They would and they did. The design they came up with was a kind of boomerang device, so shaped to take the splayed out legs of the spina bifida children. What did the boys think of the work?

It was one job I wouldn't have to take home when it was done....

... we knew it was a serious job. Dead serious.

We were going to organize the job ourselves.

We were allowed to think out our own ideas.

My mate was going on it and I went with him. After a bit I was glad I went on it.

We were very pleased with our efforts and congratulated ourselves on producing something that was really worthwhile which would be so helpful to children less fortunate than us. We enjoyed working a factory day, particularly as we knew what the end product would be and that some parents of spina bifida children in our locality had already been inquiring about our trolley.[52]

No doubt the boys in Edinburgh also thought of themselves as doing something 'serious, dead serious'. They were doing something which utilized their new scientific knowledge. In just the same way the boys at Crewe found how craft also has a social application beyond the production of toast racks and coffee tables for Christmas presents.

Someone will now point out that there is a place called the Disabled Living Foundation, where physically handicapped people can find all sorts of devices to satisfy their every need. No doubt there is also a place where anti-hypothermia devices fill the shelves. The point we are trying to make is that if Crewe has spina bifida kids, then Crewe's school kids can help them and have done so. And if Newton Abbot and Norwich want to tackle their spina bifida problem their way, well, why shouldn't they? For 'we' must take back our functions. Every school can be the disabled living foundation for its own area. By taking this function it can make education serious, meaningful and relevant for the academically inclined and those who aren't, often contributing their particular skills to the same project. At the same time the school can provide service for the community just by letting youthful ingenuity and enterprise spill out at the seams instead of bottling it up and repressing it. At the moment the really worrying thing is that most children have never *heard* of spina bifida or hypothermia and certainly they have no idea that they can do something about them. The breathing apparatus and the trolley are two items that can be produced by young people. Mothers housebound by a handicapped child need a service from young people. Television programmes show us sad tales of women who cannot leave their handicapped children for more than fifteen minutes at a time, yet are turned down when they apply for the 'constant attendance allowance' of £5 per week to which they appear to be entitled under the 1970 Chronically Sick and Disabled Persons Act. It is the function of government to support women like this financially. It is the function of the community to support them in every other way. Perhaps some straightforward 'baby-sitting' offered by local schoolkids might make government penny-pinching a little easier to bear. Old people prone to hypothermia need a service from young people. They need someone with the imagination to block off the draughts coming in their doors and through their floorboards, and they need someone with the determination to find out how that heating allowance can be claimed from the local Department of Health and Social Security (or is it from the council, or from the Post Office?). Volunteers in Islington interviewed 800 old people in February 1972, and 81 per cent said that they would like someone to apply for the heating allowance on their behalf. Ingenuity and enterprise are desirable qualities here. Have you ever applied for anything from 'them'? It is quite funny to imagine a gang of fourteen year olds testing their mental agility against the supplementary benefits system. They'll find it more interesting than trying their physical strength on the phone boxes outside the Post Office.

There are plenty of services which a school could provide for its local community, and many of these can be provided by secondary schools as they are organized at present. They would be improved both in quality and quantity, however, if they emanated from a school which was a real focal point of community life. In the previous chapter we mentioned Meals on Wheels. We know that there are children and teachers of Home Economics who would love to have a go at providing Meals on Wheels. What more realistic and practical way to teach and learn Home Economics than by planning and making meals, not only for local 'old folk' (delivered, naturally, by electric powered, non-polluting 'meal-floats' designed and built by college and school engineering and technology departments), but also for snack-time in the playgroups run by the school, and wholesome packed lunches for groups at work on environmental projects? But, as far as the meals on wheels are concerned, the WRVS or sometimes the Social Services Department itself, have cornered the market. This is not a slur on the former, and we imply no criticism of their work when we suggest that schools tackle it themselves. Ideally, of course, we should all of us cook for the person next door or down the road. For the community school, the old people of the community are all next door neighbours. Drawing children from a neighbourhood will mean drawing their families and their neighbours too, to the school. And the *doing* of this service provides the real education.

The most familiar objection to this idea goes: 'Okay – but what happens in the school holidays?' Two things might happen. The school kitchens, like the rest of the school, could and should be open and ready for use in the school holidays. They should be used by the children and by their adult colleagues who wish to join in. Secondly, if education is for real, what is learnt in term-time should be applicable and continuable at home. So the meals can be prepared at home, for the person who is now next door or down the road in fact. The whole scheme can start in a small way. Here's a conversation we had in Bournemouth with a very charming lady from the WRVS:

'Do you and your colleagues happen to know the birthdays of the people on your round?'

'Well, no, but I'm sure we could find out.'

'Here's how children can be of service – let them find out the birthdays and then let them, in school, produce staggering, individually-made cakes with things like "Have a great eighty-fifth, Charlie!" iced on them. And then let them deliver the cake in person on the birthday, with the meal.'

She thought it was a very good idea. In a small way like this community based meals on wheels could begin.

We have said rather often already that the possession of a skill, however mundane or trivial that skill might appear to be, is the key to the community, as well as the institutional, lock. And the school is a hotbed of these skills, from cake-making to advanced technological know-how. But the voluntary group has come into being in many cases, has catered for the need, and has itself become an institution. This does create a problem, and an open-minded approach to the school's new role is needed from both those in education and those in the voluntary, statutory and institutionalized field outside. This may not even be a possibility. A true community school may be too great a threat to the established cliques who look after our welfare to allow them to countenance such a challenge. We want it to be quite clear that the changes children can make may have to be subtle and small at first. Many of them may be happening right now, as kids infiltrate hospitals to be with the people inside. We should like them to see this almost imperceptible movement of outsiders into the institution as the beginning of that institution truly belonging to the people of the community. They are the vanguard, and they must remember, whenever they come across a 'staff only' notice, that from one birthday cake can grow a whole meals on wheels service if you like the idea enough.

What other ideas? The exploits of the school who invented the 'baby snatch' alarm could fill a few chapters. They have come up with an alarm clock for the deaf, and liquid level indicators for the blind, so that they will know when to stop pouring out their tea or when their milk is about to boil over. The children had to think very hard about what it is like to be deaf and blind. That is an extremely educative exercise, leading to the appreciation of greater problems than immediately leap to mind when we help a blind man across the road. How do you do your washing, when you can't see? Or buy clothes? Anyway, Walkden Secondary School, Manchester, have thought about those things, and one must admit that in doing so they have probably learnt to understand blind people better than we do. Which seems to be a sign post to a slightly improved society. Their most stunning invention was a device to summon help to a person in distress. Most of us can remember stories from the local press which were not, one hopes, quite as ghastly as one which was reported widely in national papers early in 1972: an old man was found, when police broke into his house, to have been lying dead for *three months*. It was a similar story in a Manchester paper which set Walkden School thinking. Suppose an elderly person does suffer a stroke or heart attack and falls down, unconscious but alive. How can help be summoned? A telephone is unreachable. Bells or flashing lights cannot be put into operation, even with a push-button device to set them off. The class soon realized that the alarm must be set off not by something that was done, but by something that *wasn't*. They thought of photometers, activated when dark fell, or thermostats which could complete electrical circuits when room temperatures dropped, but these were ruled out because of excessive expense or complication. Could a simple time-switch be the answer, working just like Mum's kitchen 'pinger' only on a longer time-span? Unfortunately the hopes for this idea came unstuck, for whereas the other ideas had a scientific lesson, this one had a human failing incorporated which itself conveyed a vital lesson. Even if the switch were situated next to the tea pot, would an eighty year old remember to reset it religiously every eight, ten or twelve hours? The final solution was quite brilliant, but it is not for us to say what it was. Instead let your school have a think about the problem and try to devise something for the old people of your community. It's a good way to learn by doing. Aberconwy School's jumbo chessman for the arthritic hands of residents of a local geriatric hospital, Halyard School's ashtrays for the local old folks' home, and a Doncaster School's wheelchair, are examples of similar ingenuity and imagination. What other skills has the school to offer, individually and as a corporate body?

School plays and concerts, debates and pop groups offer a good deal that's worth sharing beyond the two performances for parents and one for the school that are usually offered. The school should start examining not only what should be put on, but where it should be put on, and whether, therefore, the production is suitable not just for the parents and school, but for the local prison, borstal, old people's home, psychiatric hospital, etc. What better use for a debate than to take it into a psychiatric hospital, where patients feel useless and no amount of extra staff will improve things? Just go and look in a 'Patient's recreation room' in such a hospital, and then imagine it full, all day and every day, with some riotous happening, be it a debate, or a film show, a bingo session or a play. Here we are, back again to education: education that such skills and interests have an enormous social use, and it is this kind of education which will allow the community to achieve in this case the ultimate – the integration of the mentally ill and handicapped into this community that we talk about. For the Minister in charge of Health aud Social Security, can, if he likes, announce the expenditure of such and such an amount to replace these archaic hospitals for the mentally ill and the handicapped with small, community-based hostels. But it won't be much use to do that if we retain our fear of mentally ill and mentally handicapped people. But concerts and bingo in the psychiatric hospital are the prelude to concerts and bingo down the road in the future. Many schools do have contacts with psychiatric institutions, but always it's 'there'. Why not return the favour some time and bring some of the patients 'here'?

Street theatre and drama display distressing signs of becoming a field in which 'Interaction' and other such companies will make the community impotent to provide for itself. For those young people (and older people) of an extrovert disposition, here is yet another way to make drama and acting useful, exciting and truly relevant. The school should be able to develop the willingness and expertise that this exercise requires, though all the school kids will first have to learn to say 'boo' to the claim that 'street drama is one of these fields that needs highly trained people, skilled in communicating'. That's a skill we all need to develop and we have seen that claim before. Entertaining people in the streets, or kids in school-based holiday play-schemes can be rigorous and demanding, but schools can do it, for we have seen them.

Developing the expertise, reorienting the priorities. These two threads we can't seem to lose in this book. To pick them up schools have to take a conscious decision. If they are to reorient priorities, then they must move away from what we might broadly call the 'academic' towards what we might call the 'social'. In doing so the 'academic' need not suffer but it will probably be seen from a different angle and with a new perspective. In describing many projects so far we have tried to indicate how they can also be used to give academic knowledge, and we will discuss this far more thoroughly in the chapters on relevant education. There is no point in throwing Milton out of the window because our particular paradise turns out to be teaching English to Pakistani boys who don't speak very much. The school must also make a decision to develop these activities which are of benefit to the community. These decisions have not been taken very often, and that is why these pages generally contain too much of our theory and not enough examples of actual projects that schools have worked on. It goes almost without saying that the school should aim to equip those, young and old, who pass through it, with the kind of education most suitable for the future life of the individual. We know that for a high percentage of those who do go through school this is not the case. It wasn't the case for us either. We must cater for the needs of the community as well as the individual through the school. And the needs of the community as well as the individual frequently coincide. Besides developing skills like street drama, the application of science to real human problems like hypothermia and aids for the disabled, and other examples mentioned or yet to be described, the school must show that willingness is more valuable than training, that open-minded amateurism is preferable to closed-shop professionalism, that community service is better than mere individualism. There is already plenty of documentation that shows how many boys and girls are gaining nothing from an education based on training, academic study, individualism and competition. Watered-down academic education is not the answer, and is liable to give those with an academic bent illusions of superiority. Neither is there much point in throwing the failures into a weak stew of social education and community service, for while both are 'a good thing', they achieve nothing if they are the last resort for the non-academics and the non-volunteers. What everyone who goes to school needs is an education based on willingness, on the development of the skills and abilities of each individual, and the growth of that individual into a community for which he has learned to care, and which has learned to care for him. Caring feels pretty instinctive sometimes, but like all instincts it needs a little nurturing. Education systems in England and most of the Western world seem designed to smash all signs of this instinct out of existence. Here are a few practical suggestions for nurturing it.

'On whose terms?' That is the title we most like to offer to audiences of children, teachers or professionals outside teaching. We have described the disenchantment of those who find themselves giving their service in ways dictated by teacher, or professional or both. Far better if the service of the school in the community is a real service undertaken in ways that young people can understand and enjoy. For too long the arguments have gone on about whether service should be voluntary or compulsory. The former, with connotations of do-goodery and the avoidance of compulsory games, versus the latter, trying to inculcate the heart when attempts have failed on the brain of the less able. Both notions are irrelevant. In a school which develops games community-style, it will be found that those for whom sport is the thing will use their interest as an applied skill in the community. There was a young man in Falkirk who told us that he and his friends went to a school for handicapped kids to play games 'real games like soccer and volley-ball'. We wondered how.

> We played volley ball and found that if our lot all crouched it made things just equal against the kids in the wheel-chairs, and if we played soccer crab-fashion, on all fours, then the same thing. . . .

Alex Brooksby, who told us about these games, also pointed out that as exercise it was better than 'the real thing'. Try it and see. However, the point here is that what Alex was doing was sport, not community service. How many more kids are waiting to contribute to community life on such terms? Very few, because PE and games, which though fiercely competitive, are not necessarily solely individual pursuits, aren't geared to this type of involvement. The sport-minded could help run PE lessons in primary schools; devise exercises suitable for nursery kids and arthritic and bedridden geriatrics; could go to psychiatric institutions and share their pleasure with the obese, institutionalized mentally handicapped; could take their PE display and trampolines anywhere, teaching others and learning a bit at the same time; could devise games for the physically handicapped. It is sad to read of schools gaining first, second and third places in the County Trampolining Championships, when down the road are hundreds of younger children eager to 'have a go'. But our champions know too much about the complexities of a double twist triple somersault and nothing about the needs of others and the concept of sharing. And the trampolines which 'cost so much money, you know' are locked up in closed schools, guarded by zealous PE teachers. Anti-social.

What are the terms, then? Well, ask yourself. Ask young

people. So you dig talking to old people? That's easy, that path is well-trodden. Or fishing? Of course, your school is helping you with that, because it may well be extremely important to you in twenty years time when, like all of us, you're largely unemployed in the 1970s sense of the word. But for us the importance of fishing is who you learn from and who you fish with and who you share school fishing equipment with. With kids from the children's home? With kids down the road who are good at casting about in their spare time? Remember that there are a few old boys about who can teach you a thing or two about tying flies or deep-casting, or perhaps your school has already recruited them as lecturers?

Or is it football? Next time you're down at the Den, the Kop or the North Bank you might try taking a friend with you – in a wheelchair, of course. Having problems? Well, if you couldn't get in; or if you could, but then you and your pal hurtled down twenty flights of the terraces when they equalized, then it's time you put the club on *your* fixture list. Try a letter to Bertie or Don

Dear Bertie,

In spite of the fact that you have just reaped £200,000 by selling George to Arbroath, there is still no entrance to your ground that allows a wheelchair to pass inside. If you just give one-thousandth of that money to our school we'll be happy to carry out the necessary structural alterations to Entrance D at cost price. Or if you are really hard up because you are about to plunge into the transfer market once again, we will do it for you ourselves through a sponsored trampoline bounce-in. P.S. No doubt you and the team will help as sponsors?

You may say that radio and TV are your interests. Here things become a little more complicated, but they help to clarify our particular point. For if an individual is to offer reasonable service here, then first the school must decide, as that school decided with its alarm clocks for the deaf and its warning devices, that skills must be developed. This means that transistors will become more educationally important than the secrets of the Leclanché cell and that Sony becomes a name as familiar as Coolidge or J. J. Thompson. The school, if it is to develop a radio and TV repair service for the community, especially for those in need, must develop its skills accordingly. Those who make their living from radio and TV repair need not worry overmuch, for the school service will supplement, not replace, for the time being, and serve those who can't afford professional charges.

St Augustine's Secondary School, in Belfast, already run a radio and TV repair and supply service for local old people. In years to come we would like to think that the school as the community focus will be the dominant provider of such service, for only it will have the time and the vast labour force which can devote itself to discovering the electrical inadequacies of circuits of ever increasing complexity! There is a parallel now. If you live in London you can get your fillings and extractions done free at the dentistry departments of the London Hospital, but of course, you have to surrender your teeth to the care of students. Perhaps the day will arrive when we lose an appendix at the hands of the sixth-form biology class! Rather far-fetched, it's true, but bear in mind the device perfected by a Californian doctor with which women can perform menstrual extraction, the best sort of birth control, on *themselves*. And at a conference of health-service administrators in London in mid-1972 the treasurer of the General Medical Council, Dr John Fry, said that too many doctors were referring too many patients to hospitals for treatment. He said that if these unnecessary referrals were dealt with outside hospital, the hospital patient intake could be cut by 20 to 25 per cent with a potential saving of £100 million. There was a tremendous scope not only for saving money but for improving the quality of care that patients receive. So here there is a case of the professional passing people to the super-professional, the hospital specialist. So often this is done because the home conditions of the patient mean that nobody can perform little jobs of caring which would enable him to stay at home, so he is moved to a hospital, professional nurses do the caring, and specialists take over from GPs. The answer again is in the community, the neighbours, the local school kids. The GP could then look outward into the community for assistance with individual cases, rather than inwards, within 'the profession'.

This, then, is the stand we take. Young people must serve the community on their own terms. Anyone in the community must serve it on their own terms. Then they are not 'serving the community' but doing what they can do, or enjoy doing, in ways and places which makes them a service for others. It is a stand based not on idle theory but on the hard experience of confronting young people with their importance to their own community. Talk about fishing and football is far more real to most of their lives than the most heart-rending stories of the underpriveleged in our communities. We believe that the powerlessness of people to penetrate institutional and community fields is a real problem, and penetration as what we are offers more hope of success than penetration as unskilled, unqualified and untrained social workers, hospital workers, play group organizers and the rest. We are appalled by those who say, 'What we are looking for in a volunteer is integrity, reliability, continuity and confidentiality....' These qualities, aside from the fact that they may be suggested because they are so extremely difficult to meet, and thus guaranteed to put many people off, may be possessed by the League of Hospital Friends Volunteers, or established bodies like the WRVS, but our young people can't begin to satisfy such terms. Some young people are tempted up the blind alley by showing others that they can compete on these terms. A good example is the research undertaken by Miss Marian Would, former director of Task Force, in Aylesbury. There she set out to prove to a somewhat sceptical team of local social workers that young people from Quarrendon Secondary School could be just as good as interviewers in a housing estate facilities survey as any professional. As it turned out, the survey went one better, for it seemed that people interviewed by schoolkids made clearer, less inhibited answers than they would have made to someone with a more impressive appearance. But in this success lay a deeper failure, for these young people, by proving their ability, became a first-class threat. The professionals entrench before a threat. Yet we would guess that in Quarrendon School there are plenty of those youthful skills, abilities and energies which, channelled, encouraged and developed, could represent, in ways that we have tried to show, much that can be utilized for the good of the community. And they could do it in a way that represents a threat to no-one.

In short, in serving our community we are none of us, young or old, to try to be mini-versions of professionals. That way we'll lose every time, for though we may make some progress, we will be branded as amateurs and forever kept firmly in our place. The jobs will be referred to us and the terms controlled by the professionals, be they planners or psychiatrists.

If we serve on our own terms we can move towards the situation where *we* do the referring. For example, if we survey the needs of the handicapped there may be needs which we, the community, cannot cater for: the installation of telephones, the payment of benefits, or the provision of certain highly specialized services. Such cases we can refer to 'them' for the necessary action. In the same way, in tutoring, which we shall describe in detail later, it might happen that the young person who is tutoring another is getting nowhere. He suspects something more fundamentally wrong than he can cope with. This is where the tutee is referred to the dyslexic expert or the psychiatrist. We look forward to the day when schools and colleges run courses in home medicine, so that we can share in diagnosis and refer to the specialist ourselves. The possibilities are endless. The local planners (us, that is), in planning our own local park, or the new houses we are to move into, will need, very likely, to call upon the advice of the professional designers, landscapers, geologists, etc. when their expert help is necessary. We are not saying that we don't *need* professionals, but that they must be at our beck and call, not vice versa.

Let us end this section on a simple, human level. This story is taken from an article written by a headmaster about the achievement of his children. It is very important.

St Anthony's community-service programme has achieved all that was originally hoped for and much else besides. Greater awareness of social needs has certainly been evident amongst the children, but, equally important, have been the opportunities available for these less able children to make a significant contribution and to experience success, thus often restoring lost confidence and self-respect. Such experiences are the best cure for self-pity and extreme introversion and lead away from 'the world owes me a living' approach to life. Dignity is restored where dignity has been lost and a general sense of well-being is promoted. It has been rightly stated often enough that we need the approval of our contemporaries and if this is true for those of us without the burden of handicap to carry, how much more must it benefit those less fortunate, to have earned, by their own efforts, the warm approval of their community? The school has also gained enormously from these arrangements; the spirit of service is continued within the school and the unsupervised maintenance of areas of responsibility has contributed not only to the development of the children involved but to the general standard of comfort for all.

But more than this, the various schemes of social aid have meant that the school has been cheerfully adopted by the city; there is no stigma in being a pupil at St Anthony's.[53]

Yes – that school was a day E S N school. Mr Maxted continues:

What a good man did on a dusty road long ago in Samaria was beyond praise, effective and compassionate. It did not, however, require any great intelligence, merely an acceptance of the fact that all men are brothers, and a willingness to serve.[54]

Here are our low-ability children setting the kind of example we would all do well to follow. It is a pity that we stand in danger of confining such simple, human and important notions as willingness to them, and fail to heed them ourselves. It is no fluke that our institutions of higher education have such appalling records of service, for too many have reached the higher academic ether entirely unversed in the kind of social understanding that the E S N children of St Anthony's gained. Who would you prefer to live with? Which do you regard as the more important educational priority?

BEEFSTEAK'S BOMBSITE
one afternoon
AND BEHIND THE SUPER BINGO-MARKET I'LL PUT A MULTI-STOREY CAR PARK....
GORILLA
TWO AND A HALF MINUTES LATER
PRESS
PRESS
SENSATION
BEEFSTEAK ANNOUNCES PLANS TO BEAT DEVELOPER AND BUILD PARK. Beefsteak this afternoon opened his park campaign....
1. To raise money for equipment by selling bombsite relics etc.
2. To get help with demolition and land clearing.
3. To protect the park from rubbish dumpers.
He said he ... support...
MAN BITES ALSATIAN
BEEFSTEAK..
Why must h shortage
OLDE ENGLISHE FIREPLACE £5
5P FOR 3 BALLS
SALESMAN
ARMY HEADQUAR
ENGINEERS
PLAN

TEMPORARY CAR-PARK
charge per day....
1 SACK OF EARTH
or..........
or..........
or..........
THEY WORKED HARD UNTIL....
THEN ONE NIGHT
THE FOLLOWING EVENING

5 Environment

So far we have been talking about the social environment in which we live. We have said that at the moment people cannot realize their potential by contributing to the social quality of life in their community. We have tried to show that the present system of central, professionalized control over our social lives does not work. The professionals often go about things the wrong way and their control means our apathy and helplessness. And the system is wasteful, because it not only does not recognize the many skills and talents we all have, but prevents us from using them. We have been saying that the solution to many of the problems of society today is people, people with power. Can the same be said of the many environmental problems with which we are faced? Are people the answer here? Since the air we breathe, the water we drink, the products we consume are all *ours*, and it is *our* environment, we believe that a very large part of the answer does lie with us. But we have to sort the subject out first of all, because environmental pollution, conservation, preservation and the rest of them have all been collared as 'problems' and their province, by new breeds of professionals. The struggle is on once more. Our environment is rapidly becoming 'their' environment, by the same processes as we have described in relation to 'community services', and we are in danger of leaving it all to them, once more.

There is no point in adding to the volumes of literature produced over the last several years about the eco-crisis and the impending self-destruction of planet earth. Five minutes of Paul Ehrlich is enough to convince us that they're right – isn't it? Aren't they? Well let's say that it makes most of us dimly aware of the issues involved. The dimness of our awareness is, however, the fault of two fatal mistakes in the methods of the pollutocrats. We do not take issue with the content of their argument, but the method. Firstly, the basic stance of the new environmentalists has been directed towards the application of pressure to change government policy. Quite apart from the fact that we can all see that many in government have a vested interest in polluting, since it usually makes a lot of money, this leaves the individual, all too often, with a 'what's it got to do with me?' attitude. That's how dim the awareness is. But let it be said that groups like Friends of the Earth have also been attempting to create awareness of the problems among individuals as well as taking a thundering, pressuring, preaching stance towards government. The two postures don't live too happily together, though, and individual awareness seems to be taking a back seat. Secondly, both government and the pressure groups trying to influence it have managed, in their professional fashion, to couch their pro and anti arguments in totally incomprehensible jargon. And jargon always reinforces the 'what's it got to do with me?' attitude. Besides this, the pressure groups themselves are in danger of becoming just another part of the bureaucracy of the environment, the alleged popular control tower, the anonymous empire to which governmental power gives a brief nod when it feels inclined.

Of course we are not saying that there is no legitimate place for pressure group activity. But it must be rooted in real popular concern, not the concern of a few who claim to represent the needs of the people. The pressure is then an effective one. If the pressure is not based on the concern of the people, it is ineffective in two ways. It is less credible – 'just a bunch of pessimistic disaster mongers' and it entrenches in the man in the street the feeling 'I couldn't care less, let them take care of it'. If we look at an example from a broader community front, perhaps the success of the community experiments in Golbourne, Notting Hill, are a good demonstration of the response of ordinary people to a chance to effect change. Nobody, not even George Clark, much as he must have felt tempted, has claimed to represent the interests of this community. The people represented their own concern, exerted their own pressure and got their own results.

Often we are told that community action and community involvement are the antithesis of pressure group activity. In the broadest sense community action seeks to provide for people through people, while pressure groups want 'them' to do more for 'us' or the homeless or the disabled or whatever. We feel that the latter pressure only works if it springs from community activities. Community involvement brings the individual some power over his own life, helps him to service other people's needs and receive help from others too. The issues that arise from such involvement, such power, need a clear, loud voice – a community pressure group. Here are some environmental issues which illustrate this point, and also help to indicate whether the environmental battlefield is in the institutions of government or the streets and gardens and fields of everyday.

One of the planks of the eco-disaster platform is the 'exhaustion of finite resources' issue. Indeed, it is one of the stoutest planks, as we are sure many more would agree if they understood the jargon. It means, more or less, that we are going to run out of things that we dig out of the earth, like coal and metals and oil, for example. And when we run out, what then? The three materials we have quoted are only examples. Think about the materials of which your house is made and you will come up with plenty more. Now there are two ways in which we can defer, hopefully prevent, this particular eco-crisis. We can use *less* and we can *recycle* what we use. At the local government level a pressure group might try to improve the processes by which the local authority deal with waste. Some authorities do separate recyclable material rather than dumping it willy-nilly. It seems that recycling doesn't have too much effect on the rates. But if you try suggesting recycling to your local authority, the most likely response will be that the rate payers won't hear of it. Try getting your council to change *anything*. The way things work at the moment, we are responsible to them, not they to us! At the local level pressure group policies are unlikely to achieve success unless the pressure is something far more widely spread, a pressure from all the people.

Community involvement in this issue, with young people in the van, can be far more effective. Many families give the younger members no very clearly defined role to play, just as they are given no role of their own in the community at large. We suggest that one of their roles could be that of recycling-watchdogs in every household. They watch the household waste. If necessary, they take it to school. It is clearly not realistic to expect every householder to drive fifty miles every Monday to the paper factory with last week's old newspaper and bags, fifty miles on Tuesday to return all the tin cans, and fifty miles on Wednesday with a load of bottles. But anyone who knows anything of recycling has a vision of it really becoming an accepted part of our daily life to separate our waste. For it to happen properly some kind of community cooperative venture is needed. We have already described the vital role the school has to play in such community ventures. Kids from schools are close enough to everybody in the community to get it all going.

Obviously the first step is the instilling of environmental consciousness in the children. Very few schools are doing this on a concerted basis at the moment. In the chapter on relevant education we give a few suggestions as to how they can improve on their record. One aspect of their environmental education, if it is to be any good at all, will be actual *work*, active projects to improve the environment. We don't want to produce a breed of morbid, do-nothing doom-watchers. Having earlier dismissed charity, we might now say that conservation begins at home. So here is an elementary scheme for action, involvement, change. Young people devise a system of dividers for their dustbins, rather like saucepan dividers. This can be done in school workshops, and it will be taken up by business, as soon as any success is seen. School workshops can beat them to it, though. Into the sections go various types of waste – paper in one, glass in another, scraps and 'biodegradeable' (decayable, compostable) rubbish in another, and metals in the last. That's four compartments, for a start. From here on one of several things might happen. The local council might see the light, respond to our initiatives and collect the components separately. Apart from the compostable waste, which they dump, as they do now with all rubbish, they return the recyclable materials to a recycling source for us. But since local authorities seem to respond rather slowly to initiatives as a rule, this may take some time, and it may never happen.

So Monday in the environment-conscious school is 'glass-day'. Sandie takes the glass segment of the dustbin to school with her.

She empties it into the school truck, and off it goes to the nearest recycling agent. Recycling agents will pop up like bulbs in spring just as soon as we want them, for this is all worth money. Nothing could be simpler. Money paid for the waste covers petrol and depreciation on school transport, and the more rubbish you bring, the more money you get. Doesn't every school cherish the thought of a little fund to be dipped into occasionally for small items – like a swimming pool? Built by the school and the community together, of course. But hold on – we want to cut down on the use of glass, not increase it! Compostable waste would be the responsibility of the council.

We believe that many people would be recycling-conscious, if the mechanism existed for them to be so. We know that young people are quite capable of operating the mechanism, given the chance. Is such an opportunity beyond us and our schools? Schools in California are already operating recycling stations on 'school-yards' (playgrounds), where the local community can bring their waste to be distributed to recycling firms.

This is just one way that a school can be a source of initiative and enterprise in environmental matters. Critics of the scheme will say that the exhaustion of finite resources is a problem to be solved by governmental action. They will say that what is needed is an Act of Parliament which obligates local authorities to deal with waste in the way we have described. They will point to precedents in other environmental issues: the Alkali Acts of 1863 and 1906, the Clean Air Act of 1968, the Noise Abatement Act of 1960. There are already acts to cover many environmental problems. There is an Alkali inspectorate which has the right to prosecute firms which do not use the best practicable means to prevent emissions of grit, dust, fumes, smoke and gases. One can go back a long way and still find these laws. In 1273 the use of coal was prohibited in London because it was prejudicial to health and not thirty years later an artificer was executed for using sea-coal in his furnace!

The point is that the artificer was using the coal despite the law. The point is that the Alkali Inspectorate are the 'toothless watchdogs' that Jeremy Bugler, the *Observer's* environment correspondent, has called then. The point is that beside cement works all over the country, houses and washing are getting a free layer of concrete. The point is that our 'clean air' is full of all kinds of junk and cluttered with indescribable noise. Are laws the answer? Laws have to be enforced, they have to be obeyed. Too many aren't obeyed because they are not enforceable. Ask any traffic warden or, we suppose, any Alkali Inspector.

This doesn't mean that a system of change by statute is entirely useless. The community will need to call upon processes of law. Those at present organizing 'pressures' often give too little thought to the people they are trying to protect and too little thought to the very efficacy of what they want government to do. The community which deals with its own problems will need law, but it will not need outside organizations. It will be a creator of norms, rather than laws.

Again, acts and statutes are political weapons, prone to the vagaries of party politics. 'Vote for us and we'll do this.' So we think it worthwhile to vote for them, since 'this' seems worth doing. But it's not only the pressure groups of the community who lobby for change. Those of big business are lobbying too, to protect their own interests. So we end up with toothless watchdogs. It can be the most frustrating sight in the world, particularly for young people, to see the many thwarted by the few with money. If the community cannot have a real say in its future by using the present institutional set-up, we believe a lot less frustration and a lot more fun lies in do-it-yourself. Local government is no different from national government: local councillors often respond to business interests for the same reason as national politicians – they own them. People are puzzled and powerless.

So forget about legislation and forget about local government. Local government should be the servant of the community. Once local government *is* the servant of the community, participation follows. In some areas, community involvement in environmental problems has actually shown how local government can become the servant of the community, and how pressure, laws and norms can be effective when they emanate from community activity. The school is in an excellent position to initiate the process, once again.

Sixth formers at North Berwick High School, in Scotland, set up an experiment to monitor the degree of smoke and sulphur dioxide pollution in the atmosphere. This seemed to us a natural experiment for many more schools to take up. The apparatus and chemicals needed will be found in nearly every school laboratory. We gather that there are other simple experiments within the scope of school laboratories for the monitoring of atmospheric pollutants. What a relevant way to learn some chemistry – a manned monitoring station in every school! And once learning is put into this kind of educational situation there is one immediately obvious educational pay-off – kids who are good at chemistry become interested in environmental problems and vice-versa. It's the birth, if you like, of a scientist conscious of his responsibility to man as well as to knowledge.

Let's imagine a school with a functioning monitoring station. Naturally as many children as possible should be involved in one way or another. Now at the monitoring station the readings begin to show an alarming increase in the amount of some particular pollutant in the community's atmosphere. Using the kind of enthusiasm and enterprise which is a skill of the young, the schoolkids trace the pollutant to one factory. The school's budding lawyers and solicitors investigate the Alkali and Public Health Acts, but realize that litigation may well prove costly. Litigation is one form of action, of course, but though an individual might take a business to court, the law is rather loaded against him, for the individual is often too poor, and the business rich enough, for a legal fight. A few sponsored walks might be organized to meet the legal costs, but this school decides against court action.

Instead, it makes the community conscious of the problem. In the kind of community school we envisage, this will be easy enough. But a contemporary school will have to launch a major campaign to draw the attention of the community to the problem. Meanwhile deputations visit the factory management. Requests for improvement rather than threats are their technique at the beginning. The management are well aware of the rising tide of local opinion, of the stories in the local paper, of the correspondence from local citizens. If they're smart they see that this contrast from the former apathy of the local community has been sparked off by the schoolkids. In the community and the school, the technologically minded, students, even people who work at the offending factory, will be working on solutions to the problem in technical terms. These, with appropriate costing, can be put before the management. There is a good chance that when the community expresses its concern in this fashion, there will be a response. The bigger the business the less chance there is of local pressure being effective. So what if no amount of discussions, demonstrations, boycotts, strikes succeed in reducing the pollution? What then? Local government now becomes the servant of the community, through community councillors who have no political background. Local government has powers to squeeze offending industry, and the community should be able to ask for their use. Perhaps the planning permission recently applied for by the factory will be refused. Perhaps the rates will be increased for that business, or perhaps extremely stringent checks will be kept on working conditions, fire precautions, etc. Life for an unpopular business could become extremely unpleasant. And if none of this works, maybe the land could be rescheduled for housing rather than industry. Or that motorway route . . .?

For this whole process to start there are two requirements. Young people must take the initiative; schools must encourage them to do so. Through such a piece of community involvement, the school's role as a focus for the community will clarify.

The water pollution problem is identical. Four young fifth formers at a school in Essex did some monitoring work on a local river. Not having a clue about how to go about it all scientifically, they wrote to local firms asking for information about suitable experiments. The information came, and the boys chose to assess pollution of the river by measuring the rate at which oxygen in the water was consumed. This rate increases with the number of bacteria present, and the number of bacteria increases as pollution, by sewers etc., increases. So to our air-pollution monitoring station we can add teams who regularly sample all local water-courses. Only schools have the time and energy to take on this 'watchdog' function. They have a certain amount of specialist knowledge, too, which can be supplemented by experts in the community, who thus become involved in the school project. To the problems of air and water pollution we must add noise, and here again the 'watchdog' function is a natural one for the school. Of the monitoring of noise pollution we can offer an actual example of a schools project where local government actually offered to serve the young people.

This happened in Islington, where the public health department asked all the secondary schools in the borough to carry out a noise survey for the department. This is a very unusual occurrence. In this case 'they' were not merely asking 'our' opinion, but seeking 'our' active assistance. It is a refreshing story to tell. The public health department in Islington needed the help of the young people in several ways. Firstly, they worked on a questionnaire, which they presented to every tenth householder in the area. The first question in the interview was always 'Are you worried by noise?' and this was followed up with questions about the source, time, degree, etc. of the noise. The completed forms were delivered to the public health department, who then recalled the schools to carry out noise-meter readings at certain locations, not only the 'black spots' indicated by the questionnaires. The young people were then asked to draw noise maps of their area, sometimes separate ones for day and night time. From these maps the planners of Islington can make more considered plans for the borough's future, especially with regard to the location of major roads and noisy industry. The whole scheme is certainly not regarded as just 'something to keep the kids occupied'. Indeed, it is the 'real' aspect of the survey which appealed to most to the girls we spoke to at one of the schools involved. Their teacher felt the same, and pointed out that the local geography of noise was far more meaningful and relevant to the girls' education than the study of the geography of the Paris basin.

Perhaps the success of this scheme will open doors elsewhere. Not everywhere will schools be *asked* for such help, unfortunately. In these cases the school must first do the survey, then get local government to take notice of it. They could point judiciously at the Islington precedent for support. So many projects mounted by schools at present almost reach the point of having a real influence, but then, shocked by their own audacity, take off in the other direction. Traffic surveys, for example, are carried out by schools all over the country. But the surveys are not 'for real' and consequently they lack credibility in the eyes of the pupils. If, like Islington, they were 'for real', to be presented to local government, to be examined in the local press, then they would have far more educational value, and more value to the community too. They would be of particular value to the community if they were relevant to pressing local issues, like noise, by-pass proposals or pedestrianization plans. In Norwich local schools who form the Young Norwich Society helped carry out attitude surveys which led to the successful implementation of a pedestrianization proposal.

Near Derby, the Meadows County Primary School took up a different issue, one that will, perhaps, show the environment is as relevant to rural schools as urban schools. On her way to school one winter morning, a pupil noticed that the hedges along the road that she took to school were deteriorating. That simple observation led to a two-year-long project for her class. Firstly the class ascertained that it was salt spread on the roads in icy conditions which was affecting the hedge-rows. Then the pupils wrote to county surveyors throughout the country asking how roadside verges were kept under control. They learnt about chemical spraying of both weed-killers and 'growth retarders'. They began to understand the indirect effects, not only of such sprays, but also of simple grass-cutting, upon insect and seed-eating birds. The spraying and cutting was destroying the birds' food supply, and consequently there were fewer and fewer birds. So far this is an account of a good educational project. But from the knowledge gained from it the school could now proceed to alert the local community to what was happening so that, once again, community opinion might be given to local government on the matter. Then the county surveyor is no longer acting in what he considers to be 'our best interests' in the matter of chemical spraying. He is responding to 'our expressed opinions' as stimulated and garnered by young people.

We are not pretending that the issues will ever be clear-cut and uncomplicated. In the case of roadside verges it is likely that farmers with fields adjacent to the roads will feel strongly that the control of weed growth should be maintained. Naturally the young people will discover this. Naturally the opinions expressed to the county surveyor will include this slice of community opinion. But is it not possible that different areas of a community might be treated differently according to their own wishes if these are extremely definite?

This 'watchdog' role is not the only one where young people can take on a leadership function. Plenty of *work* has to be done, in the practical sense, by willing pairs of hands. Here again young people can provide a lead. We believe that such programmes of practical work to improve the environment will be most successful when they derive from a genuine concern engendered by relevant environmental education in the school. It is worth here remembering an earlier point about making full use of the skills and abilities of young people. We can think of nothing more soul-destroying than litter-clearance schemes where young people, like it or not, spend time clearing up other people's junk. That smacks of using juvenile delinquents, the young unemployed and the early leavers to clean up the mess made by adult delinquents. Again recalling an earlier point, if service is to be neither voluntary nor compulsory but natural, a sharing, or doing your own thing with and for your own community, we know that there are many people, young and older, who shy away from the kind of social involvement described in the previous three chapters. There is nothing wrong with this, it is merely a question of personality. For personalities who do not dig conversation with people they don't know well, who are quiet, maybe just like to be on their own, practical environmental projects such as those described here may well offer the right setting for service. In the environmental field the skills required will be different. Builders, quantity surveyors, handymen, drivers, gardeners will be needed to supplement those whose enthusiasms are botany, zoology, geography and geology. There will be demands for technical invention, and for those willing to risk life and limb by testing their swimming ability in waters considerably murkier than the local swimming bath. To these add people who like 'messing about in boats', outdoor people in general, from fell-walkers to Sunday afternoon strollers ... and these skills and interests are only the beginning of a long list.

There are those who will point out that volunteers are just 'cheap labour'. There always are. These are the same people who claim that volunteers are positively misused as 'gap-pluggers' in mental hospitals. We say once again – why worry? What is wrong with cheap labour? Anything which people do for one another and for the advantage of the community they live in can be described as cheap, for it costs neither giver or receiver anything. As we have been in these fields, social and environmental, it is often difficult to find areas where community service is possible due to the reluctance of professionals to allow 'outsiders' in. But once such areas for participation are secured, one finds 'gap-plugging!' and 'cheap labour!' hurled from every side. It is often the organizers and teachers of young volunteers and school kids who make these objections. The kids themselves just get on with the job. Gap-plugging and cheap labour are not faults in schemes of community involvement. They show that the community is servicing itself, exploiting its own talents and doing things on the cheap, to boot. It is looking after its own problems. The gap-pluggers and labourers are having a good time, allowed at last to do something useful and enjoyable. Nobody has any right to criticize that contribution.

What we do take issue with is the 'shunting' process, where volunteers are shunted off into meaningless, peripheral jobs, which take no account of what the individual has to offer, which they don't enjoy, and which don't help anyone, even indirectly. At the same time, jobs which really need the involvement of the community are denied to it. Traffic surveys destined for the waste-paper basket and volunteers denied access to people in need fall into this category.

We have gone into this here because litter clearance schemes are often branded as 'cheap labour' and 'doing the job the council should be doing'. So what? The litter problem affects the whole community. It is certainly not a meaningless and peripheral job, therefore why criticize it? What is important is that people involved in the clearance are naturally involved, because they are concerned, or because it gives them an opportunity to make use of a particular skill. Compulsion to any task breeds revulsion.

Boys at Springhead School, in Kent, undertook what might be described as a 'classic' litter clearance scheme, and local government responded to their initiative, even if only in the form of providing lorries to take away the collected rubbish, and providing some trees to plant. The scheme began from a classroom project on pollution:

... it did not seem good enough ... to treat pollution as simply a cosy academic exercise....

The actual clearing was, of course, hard and messy, though not revolting work. Wet paper was difficult to handle. Other kinds of rubbish found included expanded polystyrene and plastic containers which never decay, parts of cars, motor-cycles ... and large quantities of rubble, tin cans and rags. Even on the smaller sites the quantity of litter was deceptive and some digging was necessary to get down to ground level....[55]

A similar scheme was undertaken by young people on a housing estate near Birkenhead. There, the poor design of the doors on the waste chutes from blocks of flats meant that many had broken open in windy weather. That brought an enormous litter problem, which was exacerbated by the casual dumping of all sorts of heavier junk. Children from a school on the estate got to work, and as they cleared, local residents joined them. So the kids, far from being cheap labour, acted as catalysts for a community undertaking. A second project was planned, and a local firm offered some huge industrial vacuum cleaners to help with the work. Here again, the council responded, but an interesting point emerged: although they could handle the household refuse, the council refuse department was simply unable to cope with large-scale littered areas. So in Birkenhead the young people were not gap-plugging, they were doing a job which no 'professional' *could* do. Litter, after all, is our responsibility.

In Southampton several schools have united to form a 'Conservation Corps', and they too have undertaken litter clearance operations. At Jarrow, in County Durham, Hedworthfield Secondary School pupils removed tons of junk from the nearby River Dene, as well as landscaping the banks and planting trees and shrubs. In London, young people did the same with the River Wandle. In these cases the lesson was clear – litter and junk is 'our' responsibility.

We showed before that 'they' cannot cope with another job in the environment – the maintenance of footpaths. That is only one field where there is scope for the school. We have seen two examples of schools undertaking large-scale tree-planting in derelict areas, Holy Family RC School in Accrington, Lancashire, and Matthew Holland School, Selston, Nottinghamshire. Here again, as with so many of these schemes, it is easy to criticize the fact that the project was confined to the early leavers. That criticism is valid and we hope in the future that all ages, abilities and people who are interested in the environment will be involved. But praise is also due to these schools, and to the local government officials who have allowed, encouraged and financed the operation. If the encouragement and the environmental education is there, many young people will relish the chance to lead the community into this new field. Local government must respond to the community's wishes in two simple ways: by opening their minds, and by providing the finance and necessary resources. The Forestry Commission and local conservators of forests have long encouraged and helped schools (by providing free trees) to do this kind of work. The more local government officials who think in the same way, the better.

The conservation of flora and fauna is a highly relevant business. It seems a pity that the leaders of the conservation movements dwell upon the white rhinoceros and the whale, unthinkingly exaggerating our 'what's it got to do with me?' feeling. But most kids have never seen a white rhinoceros or a whale, even on the telly. There are organizational problems in the conservation field, though, for the British Trust for Conservation Volunteers is active here. They are short of cash, so volunteers have to pay to serve in their work camps and protect nature. And you can't join up if you're under sixteen. So here is that old exclusivity poking in again. This is not for the young, only older, stronger 'conservationists'. No wonder kids shrug their shoulders and heave their Pepsi-Cola tins over them. They can't conserve till they're sixteen, and anyway, what does their education tell them about conservation?

Quite a lot if they are lucky enough to go to Archbishops' School, Canterbury. Some years ago now, the fourth year rural studies group were introduced to the sphagnum moss bog at Hunstead Woods, six miles from their school. The Kent Nature Conservation Trust had been asked to save this peat bog from drying out, and they had the foresight to enlist the help of Archbishops' School. Since then, this has been the school's responsibility. Clearing the encroaching birch trees, digging drainage ditches, building bridges, clearing paths, making seats, studying wildlife, experimenting with the best conditions for the growth of sphagnum moss – the boys have been busy with all this. On the way they have investigated the historical uses of this interesting natural phenomenon, a moss of very great absorbency. This has led to experiments on its chemical properties, and the boys have discovered a definite tendency to reject bacteria. Mathematicians have surveyed the bog, with home-made equipment, and mapped it with accuracy. There has been a role for many skills. One wintry day the rural studies master was amazed to see boys working with great zeal, carrying rubbish to a big bonfire. When he investigated he found that the boy in charge of the fire was cooking sausages and putting them in hot dogs for the workers! Now this master was a teacher of many years' standing, used to the rigours of work with bored, frustrated 'early leavers'. He confessed that he had been dubious at the beginning about the workability of the project. After all, boys who played truant with no encouragement at all would be working half a mile away, without any supervision, on the other side of a wood. This teacher was amazed at the way his fourth year took to this responsibility. And almost speechless when an examination, which he gave after about six months work on the bog was marked. The improvement in the written work of the group was quite unbelievable, and the actual answers to rural studies questions (slanted towards sphagnum moss bogs) outstandingly accurate. Add to this the fact that the boys cycled six miles to the bog and six miles home, and often worked after school time, and suddenly the educational value of environmental projects hits you right in the eye.

So the fact that organizations don't accept under-sixteens because they consider kids incapable of the work seems particularly ridiculous. Here the organization is almost fitting the 'professional' pattern, with exclusive rules of entry. Conservation, if it is to succeed, must not be for 'conservationists' but for all of us.

The next example reveals a whole new field, the prevention of dereliction of both land and buildings. A school in Skegness has played a valuable role in preserving and maintaining a windmill.

While the external appearance of the mill is the responsibility of council staff, the interior has been renovated and maintained by about 150 boys and girls from Morris County Secondary School. So here not just early leavers were involved. To attract visitors, the boys and girls labelled the parts of the mill's old machinery and in a nearby building they have established a windmill museum, containing maps, models and information about mills, particularly in the Lincolnshire area. This museum has now overflowed into the car-park of a nearby restaurant, for local farmers have given the school an old cart and farm machinery, which has been painted and restored by craft classes from the school. Other associated projects included a taped interview with one of the last millwrights left in the country.

There are schools which have undertaken similar preservation activities through the Schools Council Design and Craft project, showing how this work in the environment is not just an outward extension of environmental education but a field in which many skills – craft, art, geography and history – can be learnt and applied in a 'real' setting. In all the instances we have recounted such learning outside school has clearly offered a more exciting, more realistic and more appealing kind of education to the children involved.

A problem which besets this kind of project is that of ownership. Whose slag heap is it that we want to cover with trees? Whose rubble-strewn piece of land that would make a fine park playground? Who owns that old building we would like to preserve? Here again the budding lawyers and solicitors and, in the community schools we keep coming back to, real lawyers and solicitors, will be able to help. It is obvious that this is another key area in which we shall need local government officials to clear the way for us. Take a hypothetical example. Young people may have noticed, during a survey, that a particular part of an urban area is chronically short of open space. Having secured the necessary information, including the result of a questionnaire on the issue, the school put to the local planning and parks department a proposal that a piece of derelict land should be made into a park. Grass seeds, plants, shrubs and bricks and mortar will be needed. But who owns the land? If, like the windmill, it's council property, there's no problem. But if it is privately owned? Well, if it is so easy at present to operate compulsory purchase orders to rebuild flats and shove in motorways, can't local government respond to the expressed wishes of the community by compulsorily purchasing this piece of land? Again, the catalyst role of the school is clear. It must galvanize local opinion to achieve change.

It is in the field of environmental matters, planning in particular, that the community's inactivity and apathy is most marked. The planners invite us to participate but reign supreme. We let them take care of everything, and we don't know how to express our thoughts, or even that we can express them. We are apathetic because we are ignorant, and the planners foster this with their own brand of jargon and secrecy. Add refuse, parks, highways and surveyors to the planning departments and we find there are just too many cases of failure to 'do it the right way' or even to 'cope'. The problems posed by our environment are immense, from preserving rare species from extinction to adopting ecologically reasonable methods of refuse disposal. This failure of the professional opens many avenues for young people and the community in general to explore, and we have attempted to describe some of them. The very fact that the environment, unlike, say, the hospital, is well and truly 'ours' makes it easier to expand the community's participation in this field. But schools must act quickly, for if anything comes from parliamentary debates, pressure group activity and UN conferences, all couched in language beyond all of us, it will be more provision, more professionals, more laws. And that means less and less opportunity for the people to keep what is 'ours', not 'theirs'. We must give our young people that opportunity now, because laws, provision and professionals are failing them too.

6 Young and Old

Divisions in our social structure are fostered and tended by our educational institutions. In a chicken-and-egg situation who is to say which came first, yet clearly the divisions are now out of hand and have split communities far beyond the 'divide and rule' concept which they once furthered. Schools divide everybody. They split families: children from parents at an arbitrary age; children from their siblings, from friends they make at home. At eleven years or thereabouts, relationships are once again severed and a whole new environment is offered, but one which contains the most marked schisms of all.

The secondary school is divided into classes, or forms. Each class contains children from the same age group. This ranges over about eighteen months, so that in the first class of a secondary school there are generally no children younger than ten and a half years nor older than twelve. The official explanation for this age grouping is that you cannot 'organize' teaching in any other way. Children of the same age are at a similar point in their learning of the ordained subjects and thus one teacher can confront them all and submit them to the same process without fear that too many will be left hanging out at the edges. Those that hang out beneath are often called educationally subnormal. Those that hang out above are sent up into the next age-grouping – form two. Unlike the general concept of a group of people which has as its core the notion of a common good for which all parts work and cooperate, a class group is, as we shall see, that paradoxical notion, a group of competitors. Therefore it presents no common front, and has no real common interest except insofar as the school organization gives it a number and a room and its members are the same age.

Everybody knows this is how schools are organized. Organization is the most obstinate barrier in talk about alternative systems of education or alternative anything. 'What about administration?' comes back from every side. Let's start by looking at the weaknesses of age-grouped classes in schools. What's wrong with that sort of grouping?

It is an unnatural grouping because it is sterile. Our most fruitful relationships are with people whose experience differs from our own. Although a group of thirteen year olds may have slightly varying home backgrounds, the connections they make in their class at school stay with them throughout their time at that school. The home differences, and often there are not many of these, are left in the background as all thirty pupils do the same lessons and the same homework for five years or so. What's to stop outside friendships? Nothing but the need for a superhuman effort to make them. Assembly, break and the lunch hour are the only regular times when children can mix, and teachers will confirm that embryonic attempts to make friendships across age gaps are often looked on with suspicion, both on the part of the other children and by the staff. The usual approaches are made by the first-former with a big sister in school, who has met sister's friends at home and feels that she knows them. They will probably acknowledge her greetings when she first arrives, but thereafter she's in form one and a junior. Ventures into different classrooms are rare. The idea that staff see such relationships as suspicious may seem far-fetched, but perhaps that is the result of their long immersion in the system. They don't expect cross-class friendships, and anyway kids come to school to learn, and the learning of those in higher or lower forms has nothing to do with one another. So can such relationships be fruitful from the teachers' point of view? No – highly dangerous, in fact, since they will most probably lead to help with homework and an unfair advantage in the form learning stakes. We remember a fourth former at a girls' public school who made friends – easier in a boarding school – with a girl in the lower sixth. This friendship was noticed and her house-mistress suggested that it was not a healthy thing and should be stopped. That is a true story and the school does not seem such an antiquated establishment in other aspects.

The little body of pupils progresses *up* the school. Note the mountain metaphor, it is common parlance in educational institutions. The higher it gets, the more established its position in the hierarchy, and the more the powers of authority are vested in it. At the summit is the most established group, the sixth form. The isolation of this group is often emphasized by the provision of a room for its use, forbidden territory for those still scaling the heights. The privileges of the group are there for all to see and aim for. They are an incentive to get to the top. A more natural grouping of children is within the structure of the family. By the very force of nature the children in a family cut across these rigid groupings, only twins presenting a similar conformity. Is a family a more effective unit for learning?

When people live together they are not driven by an urgency to cram in the next chapter during the forty minutes before break. They know one another well enough to appreciate that at times a person feels receptive and wants to learn and at other times he doesn't. If you attempt to enforce learning against the will of the pupil, he becomes rebellious, you become frantic, and forty minutes are wasted in misery by both parties. However, teacher consoles himself with the thought that at least some of his thirty-odd pupils were in a learning, receptive mood, and so the rebels are condemned even deeper because they didn't conform. Class structures have never allowed the teacher much chance to deal with the feeling of antipathy to the lesson he comes across every day. It is a feeling most people have most of their lives: an unwillingness to do what other people think they should. Discipline has long been the answer in schools. Yet, disciplined though we may be to sit silent and look as if we are learning, if we don't feel like it, we don't learn. Teachers have moods too; where they don't feel much like communicating. Those lessons are really dreadful. Where people know one another much better than teachers know pupils, they can cope with one another's moods. They can understand that a person who feels like learning and is in a good situation to do so can absorb with critical understanding enormous amounts of information in a minute portion of the time allotted in school for teaching him. But such situations present themselves only when teacher and pupil are sensitive to one another's moods and personality and have a good deal more of one another's lives than forty minutes before break to share.

A mixture of different ages have many points for interaction. Any mother-and-baby book will tell you that second and later children will often learn to speak earlier than first children because the older children teach them, not in a formal way, but simply by being closer to them in experience, by being on their 'wavelength'. Often, too, similarities in the qualities of voice tone amongst young children mean that the baby understands his brothers and sisters better than that enormous animal, his mum. Conversely, one sometimes hears that a baby did not learn to speak until far later than his brothers and sisters, because they understood his needs so very well that he didn't need any words. What a magnificent lesson in communication that is! Perhaps, in the end, more important than learning a language from one's family, learning that language isn't essential to understanding.

Learning at a very early age is especially noticeable because so much is learnt in such a short space of time, and not a professional teacher in sight. What of later on, when so much of the function has been taken over by the institution, what can other children teach then? Perhaps one of the subjects about which most is written, with no effect at all on children, is sex education. In any extremely private and personal area, children are particularly embarrassed by the clod-footed tread of their teachers and their parents. Some of the most reassuring bits of knowledge about sex most of us glean come from other kids, who know a bit more than we do. The information may be off the beam conveyed in startling rhymes and jokes, but something filters down. It may be an inadequate knowledge, but it is a necessary supplement to 'lessons' on the same subject. Essential to this natural communication system is a freedom to mix and discuss with those who know that little more, generally our peers, or those a little older. Sadly this is often difficult, particularly for children from small families, and teachers are taking over *that* responsibility completely, too.

Other areas, still rather private ones, in which interaction between children is very fruitful, and sometimes the only possible interaction, are those of the imagination. This may sound pretty frightening stuff to educationists, especially the progressive types, out to nurture the latter quality for all they are worth. We have the word of some of the most distinguished of them that kids just do not *think* like adults. It's not that they understand *less*, they understand *differently*. There are all sorts of clichés about the world of the child, too many to shrug off. The development of imagination is so delicate a matter that it can really only be entrusted to those we choose. Within the rigid school structure we can only choose from thirty of similar age or that bloke up the front, of course. But he hardly seems a welcome repository for our painful burgeonings. He's just there telling us what to do.

We seem to be building up a case for age liberation on a par with Women's Liberation. Don't forget that in some institutions the division is not into classes of similar age alone, but of similar sex too. But that is too absurd even to think about, surely? Does age division stop at school? Certainly not for those who enter the foothills of 'higher education'. Three or four years incarcerated in institutions with hundreds of other late teens/early twenties, as the magazines say. Who can blame the young graduate or teacher who looks out over the great chasm of society into which he is about to leap for the first time at twenty-one or twenty-two, for feeling scared. Scared? With all that education behind him? Surely the least we can offer through our education system is a little confidence to live with other people. Yet can our most highly educated or 'schooled' young person go out from his institution to communicate (the verb from community) and live fully amongst a whole variety of people? Well, usually, he can't. Usually he chooses his friends from amongst graduates, usually from the same disciplines, and usually of the same age.

His education, plus economic pressures, will lead him to live amongst similar people, and his whole social outlook is defined by the narrowness of that formalized class one. Is this fair as a generalization? Certainly every twenty-five to thirty-two year-old graduate doesn't live in a ghetto of twenty-five to thirty-two year-old graduates. But have you ever visited one of these quite smart housing estates in the more salubrious big-city suburbs? Any pensioners there? Any teenagers? None of the former, seldom any of the latter either. The set pattern is a young wife and two or three kids. The pavements outside are littered with tricycles, and the lounges inside with coffee cups. The possibilities for interaction are extremely limited because experience is so similar. There is no need to trace the development of other age-ghettoes right through to the old-folks' maisonettes. The point is that they are recognizable, they are common, and as communities, though they may appear to have potential on the surface, they are barren. The most vibrant, exciting and cross-fertilizing groups are those with varied elements. The most exciting areas of a city are the most cosmopolitan. This extolling of differences is getting out of hand, and is liable to lead to thoughts about racial differences in schools. What exciting points for growth these provide, if they are allowed to. Unfortunately they usually aren't, because we are scared. Scared in the same way that the young couple are nervous of buying their first house in the street that seems full of middle-aged couples and old ladies. There are no young children for their own to play with. (Why can't young children play with old ladies; they'll find other young children when they want to, since children can be divining rods for one another.) And so, with the best intentions, they choose to live in a group with other young couples of similar age and the segregation process continues, inexorably.

Once you have only limited outlets for your discovering mind, once your neighbours, and those in the next streets, and in most of your part of the town, are predictable to you, where do you go from there? It seems that frequently, having created a position of comfort and security amongst recognizable and similar families, we protect our position. We become extremely chary of unusual elements. Sometimes we say that the fear people have of black neighbours is explained by the effect it will have on property values. But often they do not own their house. Or we say that they are old, and are afraid of change. But take any group of 'likes', people of similar age, income, status and we find that they automatically band together when an invasion looks possible. The invasion need only be from someone who does not exactly obey the conventions of the group.

In this way, even after school, the notion that people of similar ages will be happiest in one another's company is perpetuated. Link this with a rate of technological growth and change which has been particularly fast in Europe in the last thirty years and we can hardly blame young people for suspecting that they have very little in common with their parents' generation, let alone their grandparents'. It is not customary for the grandparents to remain in the family as an integral part of it in this country. Consequently the average schoolchild does not have much first-hand contact with the process of aging. As with anything we don't see at first-hand, we are inclined to think that it isn't really anything to do with us and the way we live. And thus we remain extremely ignorant about ageing and about old people. They are a strange and irrelevant phenomenon to us, and as with all such phenomena, we are hesitant and ill-at-ease when we do have contact with them. Successful communication with old people often means that they have a real understanding of us, and a genuine interest in us, rather than vice-versa.

For the sake of argument we state this case in universal terms. The fact remains that many young children have little to do with older people and care to have even less. So what? Well, a whole gamut of emotional experience is denied to us if we fail to see ourselves as a part of the ageing process. *King Lear* is hardly worth a glance if we'll never be old, just as *Samson Agonistes* is hardly relevant if sight and trust were not such delicate mechanisms. It would not be exaggerating to say that the appreciation that our old people are us and we are them is a fundamental piece of learning which is not directly teachable.

It is a piece of learning which drops explosively into open minds. The point of detonation might be a reading of *King Lear*, perhaps. But is that old man effective and moving if we do not recognize his quirks? Old ladies carefully apportioning bits of jewellery and sentimental possessions: giving them away now, because they want to see the effect of the gift, want people to be grateful to them. Soon they won't be able to see it, won't even be missed. . . . Lear is important because his dotage is just like theirs and he moves us when we feel this connection. The pupil reading *King Lear* for his A-levels may well be able to discuss how many times 'Nature' appears in the play, but that play won't change his own nature much if he fails to appreciate the old everyman in King Lear. And then there's Polonius, Falstaff . . .

In less 'advanced' communities, old people play a far more important part in the lives of young people. They are 'experienced' so they can offer advice. The young mother-to-be goes to her mother for advice, but as her mother is often preoccupied with her own latest baby, it is frequently grandmother who stays through the labour and delivers the child. No need to point out that in Britain today this particular field is so tightly in the grip of the professional that even the husband is often not permitted to be present at a delivery. But in a developing country, grandma has not only reared her own family, she's been in on the rearing of countless others. And her advice is not tossed aside with a reference to the latest child-rearing techniques but valued as the words of experience. Of course, in those countries the people are so backward that they still breast-feed their babies, so what can you expect when they listen to old wives' tales.

In his paper *Education for Self-Reliance* Julius Nyerere discusses the tendency of the academically educated to value only 'book-learning' and technology, and to despise traditional methods. A very wise man himself, he says

> our young people have to learn both a practical respect for the knowledge of the old 'uneducated' farmer, and an understanding of new methods and the reason for them.[56]

And perhaps, with the mutual respect that grows from such a situation, the young student will be in a position to explain some of these new methods to his grandfather. We baulk, however, at being told what is right by know-alls be they seventeen or seventy, and so the essential for any real diffusion of knowledge must be a relationship. Young Tanzanians have grandmothers and great-uncles living all around them. Young Britons, as we have seen, often don't know any old people at all. It must be a function of education to provide the opportunities for these potential learning relationships to occur.

The most rigid age-division is between those who can work and those who can't. Just as maturity is a figure on a form rather than a state of mind so retirement comes at sixty or sixty-five whether it is welcome or not. This is for the sake of organization of course. We read of octogenarian actresses, philosophers, inventors and we sit back and say 'isn't she wonderful', forgetting that other octogenarians might have carried on wonderfully, too, but for the last twenty years they've been pensioners. Actresses, philosphers and inventors may be self-employed or belong to enlightened professions, or just be considered necessary. But they are not of the mainstream. In the mainstream, sixty to sixty-five means you are old.

To imply that all old people are dissatisfied with this situation is unfair. But it does seem rather narrow to assume that everybody wants to wind down towards the inevitable end. It is a general assumption, however, which leads organizations to be chary of employing pensioners, even in areas where they could be extremely useful, because they consider they will be slow, forgetful, or liable to sudden illness. However, we have, due to the advances of medical science, an ever-expanding 'old' population. No longer an integral part of the family unit, where do these people do the 'winding down' we are so sure they all want? Usually living as they have lived before, only much poorer, until the 'winding down' process has gone so far that they can no longer do so. Then they are either admitted to general hospitals, where doctors tear their hair, because they need the beds, or to old people's homes, which are the supreme instance of throwing people together because they have age in common. It would be interesting to fathom just how much our filing away of the old depends on our own age-orientation. Surrounded by our peers, old men of seventy belong to another planet, irrelevant to our lives. The old men of the simple village community, who are elevated on 'retirement' to the role of advisers to the rest of the community, are a continual reminder to younger men of the position age will help them attain. But in our developed society we choose not to be reminded of impending old age.

It is widely recognized that the situation of many old people is highly unsatisfactory. Perhaps because not so long ago or so far away they were and are cared for by their children, we nurse quite a guilty conscience about this situation. We have surrendered the task to professionals, as usual, but it is an area in which their shortcomings are more apparent than in some others. This is partly because the old are still, thank goodness, a lot more vocal than the mentally handicapped, for example, and because there are many more of them. It is also because their problems are exacerbated by their poverty. Now whenever we discuss the question of ageing and young people, this always comes up, and rightly so. Can you hope to improve the lot of the old without lobbying for higher pensions? Well, of course, more money is essential. Yet after every budget, when pensioners get a minute increase or none at all, the man-in-the-street, as interviewed by popular papers and television programmes, is appalled by the size of the pension and expresses his willingness to pay more tax if it means more money for old people. And there are numbers of groups pressuring constantly for bigger pensions, and the media give the question room, and what happens ... nothing. This is a story from a local newspaper.

Sevenoaks wants cheaper fares for its old and disabled ... and the town is prepared to pay higher rates to achieve this. This was the message that came over loud and clear at the weekend when 130 youngsters from every school in Sevenoaks took part in a massive canvas of the town.

They posed the question: 'Are you repared to pay an extra 1p on your rates in order to allow cheaper bus fares for the old and disabled?' From 3333 local residents the reply was 'Yes, we are.'[57]

The paper reported that the local council, who had previously decided not to implement a system of concessionary fares, had been forced to reconsider the question. *Six months* later, when they did get round to reconsidering the matter, a concessionary fares scheme was again rejected – 'for economic reasons'.

So there we are, with our problem. It worries us, sometimes into action like that described above. This was an excellent attempt on the part of young people to lead the community to a change. The attempt was thwarted. Sometimes it may succeed, but the time it takes authorities to respond to these initiatives is in itself frustrating to people, not just young people. It is hard to see oneself as an agent of change when change is such an elephantine process. Therefore, as well as giving our young people the opportunity to influence local and national government, we must allow them to supplement this with the chance to effect changes in an area closer to home, for the old people in the direct vicinity of their school.

Community service by young people usually begins with old people. They are ideal material. Recognizable because organization has their names and addresses at its fingertips (it actually ordained them at sixty-five, remember), one of their most noised problems is 'loneliness'. Now loneliness is something that many teachers on community-service projects feel can be dealt with by their kids. The solution to loneliness seems simple; it seems to be some visitors. So, armed with lists of old folks and lists of fourth-year leavers, the teacher pairs them up and waits for the relationship to gell.

Many teachers take far more care than this in finding out about the old people on the list and matching them with their visitors. But by outlining the procedure as we have done, we hope to bring home the absurdity of it. There are so many questions to ask: is the loneliness of old people the loneliness of not having people around? Isn't it combined with a feeling of uselessness? And isn't the 'uselessness' driven home by the visits of school community-service groups? We know an old lady of eighty-seven, who regularly receives visits from two boys from the local grammar school. Gardening is her hobby and her garden is beautifully kept, but the two boys are sent to help her with her garden. Usually they mow the lawn, and then this lady tempts them away with a sigh of relief from her garden, for a cup of tea. She has told us that she rather dreads Thursday afternoons, but she always tries to find something for them to do, poor boys. See how she reversed the roles that the visiting project assigned to her and the boys? They were sent to help her, she helps them, by providing them with work to do. It looks as though the situation has shaken down into a useful relationship on both sides. Both the old lady and the boys feel they are helping. The boys are helping her with her garden; she feels she is helping them by letting them work in her garden. What is sad is that these feelings of usefulness are based on a lie. The old lady would rather the boys *didn't* do her garden. The boys wouldn't want to do it if they knew her feelings. Certainly both parties enjoy the cup of tea they have after the gardening. She likes their company and they like hers, for it is based on mutual help, even if rather farcical mutual help. This individual case shows the dangers in the 'visiting and gardening for old folks' that appears in every report of every community-service course, club or organization.

A very slight change of attitude could put the relationship

between lady and boys on a firmer ground. The boys attend a grammar school. They study academic subjects for examinations, and the service they volunteer on Thursday afternoons is on the school timetable as an alternative to the Combined Cadet Force or clearing the school grounds. They do not learn gardening at school, and because of their ignorance of gardening they make a pretty hopeless job of Thursday's community service. And yet, if they *did* learn gardening, what a magnificent resource they would have to call upon – their friend, a fine gardener with years of experience. And how she would enjoy really teaching some young people. In this way she would become part of their learning experience, rather than time out from it.

We questioned these two helpers. Did they feel that there were any ways in which the lady they visited could help their education? But they looked rather taken aback, and said no, because they were doing physics, chemistry and maths at A-level. Did they visit her at other times beside the prescribed Thursday? Well, no, because they lived on the other side of the town and were actually very busy at the moment because of their A-levels. All agreed that they liked one another and enjoyed their Thursday conversations. 'She does go on about her grandchildren, a bit,' they said, 'but except for that she's very interesting.' A moderately successful attempt to bridge the age gap on Thursday afternoons.

Besides gardening and visiting, another activity is commonly undertaken by schoolchildren for old people – decorating. Physical and financial limitations often prevent a pensioner from having the clean and decorated house they might wish. There are sources to finance decorating materials; however, the main ones are Social Services Departments, the Council of Social Service and the local Old People's Welfare Committee. Schools often start their own fund-raising scheme to finance a decorating project. The labour is free, of course, as the work is done by the young people themselves. A good idea, and great fun, its present realization has drawbacks. Schoolchildren are often not very good decorators. There are a plethora of painters in the team, and not too many who can hang paper. Usually they manage, sometimes the results are a bit messy. A pity a local painter and decorator couldn't be asked along to give advice?

If schools were a little easier to get into perhaps we should find more than one who would be willing to help in a decorating team. And the thought that decorating teams might contain representatives from other age groups presents many alternatives which decorating activities at the moment do not. First of all, decorating becomes a learning situation. The skilled worker can pass on a very relevant practical knowledge to the children. He can use his own, often unexploited teaching abilities. The habit of decorating teams being composed entirely of children – a limited age group – will be broken. The broader front which such a mixed group offers will be easier for the old people to mix with and understand. It will be less off-putting than 'a gang of kids', and becomes a gang of people, although most of them will still be kids. The effort becomes identified less with the school and more with the community.

Many old people express fear of school decorating projects. They prefer not to have them in their homes because of the disruption they bring. Undoubtedly this work is often disruptive just because of lack of thought. To undertake such an invasion of privacy, productive as it may turn out to be in terms of friendships formed and goodwill spread, children must appreciate that some groundwork is necessary. The old people must *know* the team who will do the work; the team must discuss with the old person beforehand how the work can be tackled with the minimum of upheaval. Skilled workers will be invaluable here in breaking the ice, in giving confidence by their knowledge of the job, in assessing just what has to be done. The most enthusiastic do-it-yourselfer makes mistakes, and certainly children will do so. But groundwork should enable them to put themselves in the place of the old person and appreciate what disruption means at his age. A mental effort is required for this sort of sympathy. When we are young, change is exciting, we seek adventure and hope for new things. So a careful preparation is needed to understand that this is seldom the feeling of old people. Since this difference in attitude seems to be a source of great friction between generations, then any easing of this friction must help understanding. In other words, practical schemes of help must be backed up with other angles on the plight of the aged, including the sort of political pressure used in Sevenoaks.

Backing up work with old people must be based on the understanding that old people are ourselves, in a condition we will eventually reach, and not a different species. Could we live on a pension? Budget it for maths, and find you can't. Check out with your old lady: how does she budget it? This may sound like another invasion of privacy, but most old people are so occupied trying to make their pension stretch that they love to tell you exactly how they manage.

'Jimmy stole a pension.' That's an objection we hear so often to 'letting kids loose' in the homes of old people. Teachers who tell this story as an objection to community service activities feel that there are the alternative courses: stop community service completely or supervise two children more closely. We would hardly be writing this book if we agreed with the first course. The second course appalls us because it means that children, working and learning outside the institution for once, are to have it breathing down their necks whatever they do. Activities in the community must be carried out by children as members of the community and not as members of the school. For once we are allowing children into the world to grow up – why curtail their alternatives immediately? Yet what can we do? Jimmy stole a pension.

Did Jimmy know how much a pension was? Might Jimmy be forgiven for thinking that £5 wouldn't leave somebody near starvation point? Doesn't Jimmy need to know just how far that £5 had to go? And doesn't he need to go round the shops to see if he could live on it? And, amazed by his findings, doesn't Jimmy need to talk about money with some old folks? After all, it might help Jimmy's appalling arithmetic. The crassest mistakes in community service seem to come from lack of a real *empathy* with the people we are working for. We feel strongly that since it is this empathy with others which constitutes real education, community service as an educational resource must start examining where it is lacking. If Jimmy knew a little more about being old, if Jimmy felt that going out to decorate was going out to do a good job rather than an afternoon's larky escape from the confines of school, if Jimmy had the support of skilled and willing painters and decorators whom he could admire for their skill – and he would, because that's something he needs – then perhaps there wouldn't be so many teachers complaining about stolen pensions.

That 'outsiders' would participate in school community-service projects may sound unlikely. On the other hand, some will say that schools already do cooperate with non-school services like Meals on Wheels and Old People's Welfare. However, their cooperation is almost exclusively with the 'professional' community servers, whose weaknesses, like those of the school, are their exclusivity and isolation. We believe, and in a limited area *know*, that many people want to participate, but really don't know how. They want to participate in an everyday, natural way, and not in a formalized, sometimes even uniformed way. Moreover, the established voluntary services have become identified with the sort of middle-class ladies who were their founder members because they had the time to do good works and had been expected to do them from their childhood. This 'middle-class' identity puts off many who are willing, but fear patronage and the feeling of being on the outside. But if opportunities to participate abound, particularly to participate alongside young people, then many will find that they have the time and wish to do so. A group of 'decorators' from a university social science club were working on some old people's houses one Sunday morning. They discovered that rolls of wall paper, which had been delivered for them to use, had not been trimmed. This job has to be done by a machine. One of the group remembered a paint and paper shop with a flat above it, and knocked up the shop keeper. Far from being annoyed at the disturbance he gladly trimmed the paper, expressed interest in the project, and was afterwards a ready source of advice, help and materials at cut-prices. So someone else was included in the operation, and it became that much more a community activity.

Authorities in institutions are often extremely nervous about the effect the young will have on old people. We remember a meeting on 'voluntary work with geriatrics' at the Hospital Centre, when we suggested that volunteer organizers be a little more ambitious in the sort of helpers they accepted. 'What about blind children as visitors?' we said. 'Oh no,' said one voluntary help organizer, 'it would make the old people far too sad to see handicapped children.'

Uncaring for the old is balanced by such amazingly patronizing attitudes. In our experience the best opportunity you can give an old person, particularly a sick one, is to lead a fuller life. And the fullest expression of our humanity is our usefulness to other people. Far from depressing old people we have found that contact with young, handicapped people often cheers them up, rather on the Confucian principle 'I was sad because I had no shoes until I met a man with no feet.' But also, when they are able to guide and assist the young person, they have somebody to look after again.

Visiting old people, then, is particularly useful if it leads to *mutual* help. And there are fields where the old can be extremely helpful, though they are rarely exploited. History classes: what is more exciting and simple to organize than oral history lessons? These are particularly valid for primary schools, and young secondary pupils, where history studies centre around the area. But, higher up the school, has any history class tapped that diminishing fund of reminiscence of the 1914–18 war? A tape-recorder and a listening ear, and there's nothing many old men would like more than a chance to tell you what it was really like in the trenches, or the General Strike. And the value of such a collection of tapes to children in years to come when there aren't any people who remember the war.

Why stop at the tape-recorder? Invite some old people to the class. They may feel intimidated, so invite a whole group. Too formalized a class will be too difficult for them to handle, so provide some refreshments in a less 'school' atmosphere. But this isn't an old folks' tea party. They've come to teach, so they are on a par with all guest speakers. The subjects they know about at first hand are many. Perhaps a retired trade unionist could talk about unions in the old days and discussion could compare and contrast their present-day role. And learning from pensioners doesn't have to be confined to history. What about those who have travelled, perhaps with the army, or for other reasons? Talks on distant places as they were could be a good lead-in to the study of the same places as they are. Relevant geography. Grandmothers became very popular recently with the vogue for crochet. Perhaps their expertise could be utilized in needlework classes. Or in other domestic fields, they could well provide exciting alternatives to the regular cooking class. And of course, old people can usually read. A school-teacher was complaining to us recently about invigilating in examinations. 'And there are old people in the alms houses by the school gates who would actually *enjoy* the change,' he said, 'not to mention the boost to their income, of a little earning on the side.'

So far we have talked mainly of the problems which beset old age which are not directly the result of poverty. One problem that is, is hypothermia. We have already described how Scottish sixth formers have used their scientific knowledge to combat this killer. According to doctors, about seventy degrees is the right room temperature for an old person. Why not a concerted campaign to check that old people in the school's area are able to live in rooms of this temperature? Children will have to learn first of the methods by which supplementary benefits for heating can be claimed from the Department of Health and Social Security. Good training this, for dealing with their own claims in later years. Then 'eating is heating'. Are the old people eating the right kinds of foods? What are the right kinds of foods? Children may notice that shopping for one is a lot more difficult and expensive than shopping for, say, four. An excellent form of service might be for the more extravert kids to approach the owners and managers of local shops to see if they are willing to provide 'one-person portions' at an economical rate, so that a person living alone doesn't have to buy large amounts of food that may spoil.

Then the school investigates and compares different methods of heating. Shouldn't kids know the differences between electric, gas, coal and oil heaters? Shouldn't they know how they work? Shouldn't they hear at school about the safety label of the British Electrical Approvals Board? And thus learning leads to action. If the old person has to use coal, how can life be made as easy as possible? Do they have plenty of fire-wood? Is the coal bunker easily and safely accessible? Can a pupil living near call in the morning to help light the fire? And if electric appliances are used, are there enough sockets? And are these easy for the old person to reach? They should be thirty inches from the floor to avoid stooping. Are fireguards adequate? Is the electricity or gas on the cheapest rate? Are electric blankets safe? How expensive is the pilot light on many gas appliances? How should you handle an oil heater? Do the Gas and Electricity Boards have any help to give? What effect does natural gas have; what is natural gas; and so on. It is an exciting subject to enter, even from the point of view of the normal school subjects. But it is geared to action, even of the most simple sort.

Many old people live in old houses. It is more difficult to keep an old house warm because there are more draughts than in a new house. The school trouble-shooters help to destroy draughts, with advice from local buildings and surveyors and materials acquired from local shopkeepers and their families. So draughty doors are sealed with felt, or foam strips or long 'sausages' made from discarded nylons and scraps of material. Skirting boards and floors are covered with old blankets and carpets, and scraps begged from carpet-laying firms. Can kids insulate lofts? Lag pipes and tanks? Well, why not? Especially with a little help from their friends, or their brothers, or mothers . . .

What we are trying to emphasize is that kids and community can act where government and authority are neglecting to act, and can take over the care of the old within the community, while they maintain the pressure for increased pensions. And at the same time young people and old people are involved in the same learning process. Of course, everybody can be involved in that process: the younger, the parents, the middle-aged. They all have a need and a right to be involved with one another in the process of mutual education.

Contact with those in need leads to our own need – to care for them. Contact with old people will certainly give many youngsters who are considered 'thoughtless, selfish and rude' an insight into a condition to which they've never related, and which they've scorned. We owe them this insight.

There is another benefit to be derived from contact across age barriers, and this is the breaking of a language barrier. It has long been recognized that class differences are emphasized by language. Bernstein shows how the working-class child is reprimanded by its mother in a way which leads to a limitation of his own word conceptions and an eventual limitation on his own use of language. This limitation is driven home by the similar predicament of all the other kids who live around him, with whom he goes to school and with whom he will grow up and eventually work. His experience and vocabulary breathe the group. He talks 'young', be he ted or rocker or hippie, or whatever. And young talk isn't old talk, and old people resent the young for their very language. The opposite is also true. But the most off-putting thing about the talk of the old is that it places such importance upon events which we don't remember and which probably took place before we even existed, and implies a condemnation of us for lacking experience of these events. Wars are a good example. How many young people are bored to tears by mention of the blitz or rationing, who might be enthralled and excited by tales of the same sort if only they were told in the proper way? This way means that they are shared with a listener rather than preached at a 'long-haired lout.' Until we allow the young access to the old in a natural way, based on mutual respect, they will not cease to be bored and offended by one another. For they have been bred into these very positions of intolerance.

7 Cooperation and Competition

'You can come in now.' Silently, boys and girls enter the room. Each knows his or her place, and finds it, to sit there and read again the eight or nine figure number taped to the top right-hand corner of the desk. The clock ticks. Teachers move along the rows, handing out papers and answer sheets, and at the same time making sure that the desks are the regulation number of feet apart. Eventually all is ready. Teachers look at the clock. The kids do, too, each isolated in his desk, waiting for the green light. 'Right. You can start now. You have three hours to complete the paper.' The teacher does not have to warn the kids about the fate awaiting anyone seen helping anyone else. After a short time of secondary school that lesson has been well learnt. Time spent helping someone else means time away from helping yourself. So the great competition is on. Some are bound to fail, but even those bound to succeed won't help them. That's life, isn't it?

This is the 'soul' of school life. This is the time that counts. Not only are the future lives of the children at stake in this examination room, but the futures of the teachers as well. One's teaching reputation depends much on how well the kids do in one's subject. A warm glow of pride comes with the results if on average the grades the children obtained were better than in other subjects. Many things that go on in school have a more or less competitive edge to them. The examinations represent the supreme, extreme example, of course. But children are not just prepared for them by slogging through every syllabus. They are prepared all through their school careers, from eleven years onwards, for the isolation, for the selfishness one needs to succeed.

Outside examinations, penalties for helping one another are still severe: 'Now children, I've marked your homework and two of the essays were *absolutely identical*. The two boys in question must think I am some kind of fool. They know who they are, so will they stand up, please? How on earth did this come about, Smith?'

Smith is the clever one: 'Sir, Jones, my friend, said he was stuck, so I let him see mine.' Jones is not so clever. 'Well, don't do it again! And the rest of you, take note . . .'

It is bad, and unproductive, for Jones to be helped in this ridiculous way. But the two boys should be encouraged to collaborate in a better (maybe less obvious!) way, rather than be warned, or worse still, punished. Cribbing has nearly the same kind of emotional overtones as caning, in schools. It means helping one another – and that's *bad.* What would teachers do, if everyone got the same marks? Examiners would have apoplexy. The selection boards would sweat blood; how would university degrees be awarded? Certificates of all kinds would add enormous weight to paper recycling campaigns. That's an exaggeration. If people helped one another with learning, they wouldn't all end up equal, but they'd be more human, less competitive.

School, call it 'education' if you like, reflects the basic values of the society which it serves. Because, in general, society is comprised of individuals rather than groups, who are, in general, competing against one another, rather than cooperating, schools take it upon themselves to prepare their pupils for this kind of struggle by basing their activities on individualism and competition. But we say 'in general' for there are plenty of good examples of the 'group' in society. Trade unions, for example; or the community cooperative ventures of which we are seeing more and more; mums getting together to form playgroups, kids getting together to battle with the authorities through the National Union of School Students (N U S S) and the Schools Action Union (S A U). While many of the groups are groups simply because in numbers there is greater strength (to do battle with the employers, or the 'authorities') this is very often no bad thing. So there is some attempt, in most schools, to counterbalance the competitive atmosphere of classroom and examination hall with a shot of group spirit. Hence the house system, with young people divided into groups, but groups which compete with one another for 'house-points' and do battle with one another on the sports field. Each house wants to win, and the members of the house less interested in this competitive rigmarole are frowned upon and exhorted to greater effort. Then there are clubs and societies: interest groupings without thought of competition. But even within these groups there isn't much 'help one another' philosophy. Team sports present an interesting compromise, since they balance the teamwork cooperation with competition against the opposition. Man has competitive instincts which need an outlet, but they often get it at the expense of other people. Nobody likes to lose, yet our schools are full of failures, because if you have a winner you have to have some losers. So our competitive instincts are encouraged in situations where someone else will suffer. Can we replace the competition in these situations with cooperation? The latter is an instinct too, but schools are thrashing it out of our kids. No wonder few real cooperative social groups exist in our society.

Much of what we have said in this book is an attempt to show how we can cooperate with one another, and with others who are in need. In this section we want to show how, within the school itself, children can be encouraged to help one another and service one anothers' needs. It's quite a harmless suggestion, really. It doesn't even mean that exams will have to be abolished, overnight. But we cherish the dream that they will go one day, helped a little by this idea, perhaps.

Once again, this suggestion means that schools must make a conscious effort to change. It is simply not good enough for schools to hide behind the alibi that they respond to the demands of society. Many teachers enter the profession because they have the desire to improve society by 'doing a good job on the kids'. Talk about problems in 'emergent' nations and you often hear the open sesame 'It's education that's at the root of things....' But your most idealistic young teachers get caught up in the rat-race, sorting children out for their destined social roles in society's hierarchy, teaching the same old lessons to a new class every year. They become school academics very quickly, forgetting those thoughts of themselves as agents of change in society, because the school becomes a society in itself. Increasingly they adopt the professional attitudes characteristic of institutions, as we have seen, and they hide behind the time-honoured excuses.

Do schools not realize that they must change? They do. They

take time, but they really do. Take sex education as the example again. The subject has existed for a few thousand years, and in the mid-twentieth century schools begin to include it in the curriculum. If they take that long to respond to the idea of encouraging children to help one another, then society, as Eddie Waring might say, 'is heading for the early bath'. No, schools aren't always as slow as that. Just look at the curriculum changes that have occurred since the Second World War. Schools changed because business and technological sectors gave the word. There were not enough scientists and technologists. This was true in the United States, as well. Hey presto! Science curricula changed with chameleon-like efficiency. Big business calls the tune. Look at the latest excitements about computer education and business studies that crop up here and there. Society becomes more and more machine-minded, so schools must do the same – quickly, once more. Audio-visual aids abound: what's it called? – ed-tech (educational technology)! What the wheel was to science, chalk was to ed-tech. Gone are the days when the school caretaker pressed a button to tune 4D into BBC Radio for Schools. Now he carts highly expensive pieces of equipment around the school. The overhead projector, costing over a hundred pounds, replaces the chalk (approximately 1p) and the blackboard. Schools keep abreast of all the latest developments, paying large sums for a device that enables the teacher to write on the wall without turning his back on the class. Discipline problems are solved overnight with this equipment!

What we propose will not cost a penny. It will reduce the burden on teachers caused by over-large classes. It will cut discipline problems at a stroke (not of a cane) and it will help to produce caring people. If you're not interested in the latter, surely the other advantages sound appealing. We represent the biggest business of all – human technology or hum tech (thinks: educational jargon always goes down well). How does that sound for a good buy?

Recently there have been developments in education which raise worries amongst educationists, and some which are considered definite improvements. Here are some of these developments, ones that are relevant to our argument. The reader may decide whether they are worrying, or improvements. They are:

the rise of the large comprehensive school with a thousand or more pupils; the increase in ed-tech; the mechanization of education; the emergence of what the press calls 'pupil power'; the decline in reading standards; violence in schools; the problem of unemployed school-leavers; truancy; drugs. Some of these reflected, or were reflected by, developments in society as a whole. But we feel that the last six may be laid at the doorstep of the first two. Though we cannot fight a rearguard action against large comprehensives (with large as the operative word) and against ed-tech, we feel that hum-tech could counterbalance the dehumanization which both promote. So let us get down to it, rather more seriously.

We remember vividly, and so, we suppose, do most teachers, our early attempts at teaching. Perhaps the most vivid recollection is of the occasion when the deputy head darted into the staff-room with 'Mr Matthews has been taken ill – can you manage 4C History? They're on the Spanish Armada.' This was no time to question the relevance of the Spanish Armada to the education of the class in question. Nor shall we do so here. Suffice it to say that in this example, which is a real one – a 'first-ever' lesson in a Birmingham secondary modern, – that after forty minutes the teacher had learned far more about the topic than the class. That was the year one of us spent teaching English to immigrant boys. Qualification? Degree in geography. Prior experience? Nil. Any joy? Yes, in both senses. In the real sense of the word, a constant pleasure from the job. In the sense of success? Yes, there was that, too, when a thirteen-year-old Sikh boy, speaking fairly good English with a Brummy accent, presented a turban as a leaving gift at the end of the year. In short, with no qualification apart from willingness, and no experience, this teacher was enlightened (about the complexities of the Spanish Armada and English syntax), he *enjoyed* himself and he was *successful.*

The main point is, however, that years later the teacher realized that in that secondary school there were several hundred other people with the same qualifications and experience who could have derived the same benefit and achieved the same results. All the English-speaking boys. They could have been the teachers; they could have learnt by teaching; they could have derived pleasure from this sort of learning, which they certainly don't get stuck behind their desks in the 'passive-learner' situation. And beyond all these important things, they could have learnt the value of cooperation by cooperating. But what this teacher missed, others have taken up.

Alec Dickson, who introduced us to this idea, says that if you talk in the United States about 'community service' it is assumed that you mean how young people can help one another. Over there, talk about our traditional form of community service, the young helping the old, simply blows their minds. For in schools in the United States community service means that young people help younger people. It's called 'tutoring'. Elsewhere in the world, and in some parts of America, it goes under different names: in Cuba – 'Each one teach one'; in the Soviet Union one whole class of pupils might adopt another class; in England the 'family-grouping' or 'cross-age' grouping found in primary schools encourages the helping relationship. A pity the secondary school abandons it all for kids from eleven onwards. You might also find it called 'Learning through Teaching', 'Student Assistant Programme', 'Cooperative Learning' or 'Youth Tutors Youth'.

The idea of using kids as tutors is not new, nor is it particularly

American. It originates in the monitoring system of early nineteenth-century schools and, we believe, in man's cooperative instincts. One of the barriers hindering the acceptance of the idea of tutoring in Britain now is that it is seen as 'an American idea'. But while tutoring is in its infancy in Britain, although Alec Dickson introduced the idea more than four years ago, there are many examples of its successful use in the States. But it is not an American idea. The idea of monitors was just adopted and accepted more rapidly than it has been in England. Since we have not seen tutoring schemes there ourselves, we rely for this account on written sources from America, and on what we have learnt from friends who work there. But we have also seen the infancy of tutoring in Britain.

We start simply, with reading and literacy. In the United States, the National Commission on Resources for Youth, under Mary Kohler, has developed 'Youth Tutors Youth' programmes. In 1971 these were in operation in 200 school *systems*. Alec Dickson saw, and was impressed by, the tutoring approach, and in the summer of 1969 his organization, Community Service Volunteers, mounted the Southall Project, one of the first summer language projects for young immigrants. It was to be followed, in the summer holidays of succeeding years, by hundreds of others, set up by education authorities, community relations officers, even universities. But all lost sight of Alec Dickson's import from America – tutoring. For the essential ingredient of the Southall Project was tutoring: young people helping other young people, in this case to be more proficient in English. Talking about the tutors, Hugh Anderson, the volunteer who led the Southall Project, said

> ... age was not the primary qualification for being a tutor ... one of our best was a nine-year-old boy who had been brought up in an English-speaking home ... the primary qualification was ... their knowledge of English.[58]

About the project as a whole, and the effect it had on both tutors and tutees, the 'pupils' of the tutoring situation he said:

> It was of undoubted use to the younger children. During this (summer holiday) period teachers often note a marked and perceptible relapse in their knowledge and use of English; (this is inevitable since the only

language they are called upon to use during this period is likely to be Punjabi). We [the project] provided at least a context in which English was the spoken language, and, at best, a novel form of teaching in a small group. Classes of thirty or forty were replaced by small units of three and four, and teachers who had not often encountered the problem of learning English as a foreign language were replaced by 'teachers' [tutors] who had recently encountered identical problems. ... Instead of being the passive recipients of knowledge [the older children] were asked to be the communicators of it. ... Language acquisition can come as much through teaching as through learning. ...

For the tutors there was another, less tangible though no less important advantage. At school they were inevitably the object of a certain amount of condescension: as slightly less well-advanced pupils, their self-confidence could be a little lacking. We attempted to change their view of themselves, and of the world. Their status, their self-confidence and their view of their own value and worth could hardly fail to have been increased by this process. This conception of individual dignity and worth lay behind the project.[59]

What happened in Southall, in the summer holidays, with immigrant tutors and tutees teaching English language, should have been taken up by schools long before now. It should have happened in term-time, with all children teaching all kinds of subjects and activities. But only a few schools responded, only a few saw the value of tutoring, so clearly described by Hugh Anderson. There are other values, too. In a New York tutoring programme it was reported that over a five-month period, during which older children tutored young children, the tutees gained six months in reading age, while the tutors gained 3–4 years. In the same programme it was observed that tutors improved not only in the subjects they were tutoring, but also in other subjects. Thus, while we are particularly concerned with the effect of tutoring on the social values of children, one can also argue the case from an academic viewpoint. Some of the other values, to children and teachers, are seen in this description:

Mr Carl Fleming's sixth-grade class at Fernwood School taught a lesson on simple machines to Miss Blanche Green's second grade in a demonstration of Student Team Action. Student Team Action is a one-to-one correspondence between upper and primary students. Students become involved in 'doing' rather than 'memorizing' and plan their own presentation, method and materials. Special ability is not a prerequisite to teaching, as one entire class teaches individual students in another. The role of teacher is changed from transmitting knowledge to the role of the helper who facilitates learning. All subjects are adaptable to this teaching method – science, math, creative writing, even physical education. . . .[60]

We especially liked the part about the teacher as an enabler, rather than as the sole source of knowledge. It is clear here that tutoring can spread to all subjects, and need not solely mean that kids who can read tutor those who need remedial assistance. But let us stay with reading and remember the rows about poor reading standards, which the researchers occasionally lob over to the teachers. Isn't tutoring a common-sense, labour-intensive solution? If there are children who are backward, surely the best qualified people to help them are other children of the same generation, who remember the problems of learning to read. The reaction to the NFER report on reading standards in 1972 was a demand for more remedial teachers and more money. It doesn't cost anything, just a little time and thought, to begin tutoring programmes. These will not just help the reading problem, but perhaps let alienated, truant-playing, violent and disenchanted kids see, like Hugh Anderson's immigrant tutors, that school *needs* them. To help other kids. Up till now school has required their attendance for no other reason, apparently, than to keep them off the streets. Look at the Southall account again

"Their status, their self-confidence and their view of their own value and worth could hardly fail to have been increased by this success. . . ."

Consider now a quote from a very different source, a newspaper account of a conversation between fifteen-year-old boys about whether young people should strike to secure changes within schools.

NEIL: . . . all the wood around that organ was made by kids in the school. If you knew that bus belonged to you, you wouldn't smash it up. But because it belongs to the school and you may get told off in the lesson, so what do you do? You go up to the lockers, you push 'em over. So the doors fall off, you think it's a big laugh. You go on the coach for a ride, so you slash up the seats at the back – because it don't belong to you. But if it belonged to you, you'd take a bit more care. You look at all the sixth formers' common rooms – not one thing in there is torn down off the walls or smashed. But you look at the form classrooms; pictures are torn down, writing all over the walls – because it don't belong to us.

JOACHIM: No, because other kids use it.

NEIL: No, for the simple reason is, Joe, it don't belong to you.

JOACHIM: It's your form room. You never smash anything down in your form room.

NEIL: Who don't? Any pictures that go up in our room, the longest they last is three weeks. They get pulled down, or if they don't get pulled down, they get written all over.

JOACHIM: Is it you that does it?

NEIL: No, it ain't me personally. Some of us, yeh, we rip some pictures, sure. The things that don't belong to us. Would you smash something that belonged to you? Would you get hold of your bag and slash the bottom out of it?

DAVE: Wouldn't you stop someone smashing up something of your own which you had part of?

TONY: I'd smash his face in.

NEIL: That's it.

DAVE: And we'd stop kids smashing up the school, if we'd got more part of it. . . .[61]

Earlier we described similar physical violence occurring outside school in youth clubs and society at large. We tried to make the point that these boys were making. Nobody wrecks something that is really his own, of which he feels a part. Tony, Neil, Dave and Joachim were discussing the issue within school. Clearly they want to feel an integral part of the school. Pathetic puppet school councils are not assisting this integration process. But tutoring might give these kids a little of what they seem to be looking for; the feeling that they are really an important part of the school; the feeling that others depend on them; the real responsibility that that entails. Above all, they must belong, and they must be needed. If school makes children feel that they belong and are needed, then it is helping to prepare them to belong and be needed by a whole community. Tutoring is an essential ingredient of the true community school. And it will involve, in that school, people who have no place in schools at the moment. Tutors and tutees will be drawn widely from the community.

Schools have an odd attitude towards knowledge. It has probably rubbed off on them from the competitive world of business, once again. Certainly schools and other educational institutions seem to have a corner on knowledge these days. And if some pioneer seems dangerously beyond the institutional pale, practising his craft, be it potting or filming, in the wide world, give him a fellowship, quick, and draw him in behind the barricades. Businesses have a paranoia about sharing information with 'competitors' or 'rivals'. For years the formula for a famous soft drink has been guarded and other companies, however hard they try, can never get it quite *right*. Of course, in the academic world, the guarding of knowledge is hardly so rigid, probably because there is less money at stake. But in the higher reaches of education a good deal of *kudos* attaches to a successful piece of research, whether it reveals that the moon is made of green cheese, or the Romans had webbed feet. Meanwhile, what of the research that really counts? The whole business is surrounded by such mystique that one feels afraid to ask if anybody had ever invented batteries powerful enough to propel vehicles at a reasonable speed, for a reasonable length of time, without recharging? Perhaps they did, and perhaps big business bought that particular secret? But even if we ignore the conspiracy theory, there seems to be an agreement amongst researchers and educationists that what they are doing is quite beyond the rest of us, and therefore need not be shared. And our experience of universities indicated that researchers weren't in the habit of sharing findings with one another too much, either. So it's very heartening when somebody like Sir Lawrence Bragg, a great scientist, can talk about his discoveries and be understood. And it's an enormous encouragement to read of the way Watson and Crick almost stumbled upon the structure of DNA. And it is very exciting to hear an astronomer describing the expanding universe. But these people are the exceptions. There is little real sharing of new academic developments with the community. There is no sharing of new educational technique and method with the community. The secrecy about these developments is usually maintained by the jargon in which they are described. But we are interested too in the way schools are now actually formulating studies which will exclude possibilities of outsiders helping young people. A public school headmaster, a pioneer of 'new maths' of some sort, has claimed that one of the advantages of the new technique is that it means parents cannot help boys with their homework. Now if there is one thing likely to widen the generation gap of the previous chapter, and increase the isolation of the school which we have bemoaned throughout this book, it's this claim to a monopoly of knowledge.

But monopolies and secrecy are features of institutions. Social workers give, as one of their reasons for not utilizing the services of volunteers, 'confidentiality'. Local authorities, even after the slightly liberalizing effect of the Skeffington Report on *Public Participation in Planning* still find it convenient to keep their redevelopment, road-widening, etc. plans secret from the public they are supposed to serve, until the last possible moment. Often they do not even allow the local press to attend their meetings. This whole tendency to secrecy is yet another reason why members of the community are often made so unwelcome in fields of community work and institutions, as we have described earlier. The danger of openness, of the sort displayed, perhaps, by those scientists who tell us about their work in such a friendly way on the television, is that it might make us feel we could do it too. And why not? And the danger to the professional, be he social worker or teacher, about exposing his secrets to us, is that we might start thinking we could do that job too. And why not?

Schools give kids a good grounding in how to keep a secret. Cribbing and sharing knowledge is industrial espionage, school-style. For school pupils, knowledge is something to be stored up and regurgitated, for exams, and tests. But instinct acknowledges other needs: outside the exam hall someone panics – he can't remember the formula. Someone will help. Possible questions are discussed. These conversations reflect millions of commonplace exchanges from our everyday lives. If someone asks you the way, do you smile but refuse to divulge the information? The knowledge is just as valid as the knowledge which schools are keeping so close. We share it naturally. Yet school doesn't encourage this natural process. You don't let anyone copy your essay; you don't show anyone your exam answer. You want to be top, don't you? Then don't share.

This attitude to knowledge has to go. Schools must see that

'knowledge is the currency of interaction' (Professor Herbert Thelen, Chicago University), rather than something selfishly accumulated in an atmosphere of competition. It seems such a waste to learn all those things and not to share them. And sometimes it seems that putting a piece of learning into words clarifies one's own understanding. Surely any teacher would be prepared to corroborate *that*?

The whole concept of the meritocratic society has been based on marks, grades and degree classes. A meritocracy isn't such a bad thing, provided it is based not on how clever you are (i.e. how successful you are in using your knowledge for yourself), but on how willing you are (i.e. how prepared you are to share and cooperate).

Here are descriptions of other tutoring programmes:

In University City, Missouri, students of Brittany Junior High School spent five hours a week tutoring youngsters at Blackberry Land and Delmer Harvard elementary schools.[62]

The tutors began by sitting in small groups and discussing what it means to learn, how they are most comfortable and when they learn; what difficulties they had, and might expect primary one pupils to have. Then, individually and in groups, they set to work at tables and desks, to prepare lessons and materials. Two boys cut paper and print flash cards, carefully lettering first-year vocabulary. A girl looks at film strips through a viewer, to decide which she could use and what kind of lesson she might build around it . . . Each child is building an abacus; he will design it and select his own materials, and perhaps later create a mathematical teaching lesson around it. . . .[63]

Here, the tutors have prepared their material, individually *and in groups*, ready for the one-to-one tutoring situation. Such a scheme was reflected in the tutoring project begun in Haverstock School, North London, in 1971. This was the work of two far-sighted teachers, Kate Myers and John Rolfe. It is one of the few tutoring schemes begun in this country. From Haverstock School, which is a large comprehensive, tutors upwards of fifteen years old went out to tutor in local feeder primary schools. They chose what they wanted to tutor, and in the six primary schools where they worked, headmasters, teachers and children welcomed them. Here is what some of the kids had to say:

INTERVIEWER: I thought you were going to teach football?

AKIS (a sixteen-year-old boy): Yes, I know, that's what I thought, but when I got there . . . !

INTERVIEWER: I bet you were surprised – you hadn't imagined yourself as being a very good teacher of little five-year-old girls?

AKIS: No, I hadn't, first of all. When Miss Myers told me about this project I thought it was just one of those things, but I didn't realize how serious it was until I actually went to the school. I had to have control of the children I was teaching!

INTERVIEWER: You liked that?

AKIS: Yes, it was great.

INTERVIEWER: Why do you think it's a good idea?

GILLIAN (a fifteen-year-old girl): Because kids of our age, you know, fifteen, sixteen – we seem to get on better with younger kids than real teachers, because they think they're great big monsters.

INTERVIEWER: Why do you think teachers are great big monsters?

GILLIAN: I don't know . . . 'Can't do this' and 'Can't do that', you know. . . .[64]

Gillian has a point. Kids associate more easily and therefore learn more easily from one another. Many teachers have realized that for years. But few schools at secondary level are producing the cross-age matching which is so important to children. Tutoring does not only cross younger children with older children, it also provides a natural platform for interaction between adults and children:

We were interested to see tutors at work in the primary schools. Staff treated them more as adults than pupils, by inviting them into staff rooms, for example, and tutors responded accordingly. The children, on the other hand, treated tutors like older brothers and sisters, using first names quite naturally. The younger children particularly were absolutely spontaneous in their acceptance of tutors – there was none of the shyness or inhibition that adults sometimes meet. . . .[65]

The secondary/primary scheme is not the only possibility. In a scheme in East London, and another in North Wales, sixth formers have helped remedial pupils in their own school and other secondary schools, with reading. In Oxfordshire we saw fifth and sixth formers, during their free periods, just 'dropping-in' to help out in the ESN class, and being welcomed.

Basically, therefore, tutoring is an extremely simple idea. All that is needed is a modicum of flexibility, so that children can move freely around the school or out of school to join their tutor or tutees; an acceptance by the school of the value of the work, both in the social and the academic sense; and staff or older pupils who are prepared to take the organizing/enabling role.

The reader can probably now guess why we have so little material from this side of the Atlantic from which to quote, and why there are so few schemes here. The reason is a perfect example of professionals banding together to prevent outsiders or 'non-qualified persons' from entering their field. In this case the banding is effected by the National Union of Teachers. They don't permit unqualified people to teach. Of course, tutoring is just another word for teaching, isn't it? To the NUT, if unqualified teachers are bad news, then unqualified *kids* working as teachers! – Heresy. The arguments we advance for tutoring go like this. First, it develops a sense of 'community' in a school, by cross-age grouping and providing an activity in which even non-academic kids can participate as tutors. Second, it avoids the cultural and generation gaps, which a teacher of forty experiences with a twelve-year-old child. Third, it encourages cooperation between tutors and tutees. Fourth, it gives the tutors a feeling that they are needed, it gives them valuable self-esteem. Fifth, it shows that knowledge has a real use: it is to be shared, to be used to form relationships. Sixth, it increases many times the amount of teaching that actually goes on in a school. Seventh, it offers some children a leadership role which doesn't require Outward Bound courses but exists in their own schools. Eight, it makes individual instruction – a cherished goal of many teachers – possible. Nine, it provides an 'army' to combat the remedial problems which confront so many schools.

How many teachers are actually *against* these arguments? Will they therefore take a lead for their profession and admit qualified tutors: qualified by their willingness? For a long time, after all, we have delegated *disciplinary* functions to children in schools: prefects, monitors, house-captains. We have also delegated certain *administrative* functions to them: ringing bells, organizing sports practices, etc. We believe children are capable of handling the teaching function.

While it is easy to imagine sixth formers doing tutoring work, because they have so much free time, it is less easy to see how other pupils can do it. Mind you, teachers may tell you that sixth-formers spend their free time in intensive study. Actually they don't. They waste a lot of it in silent libraries, staring out of the window! But at least, if they wish to tutor, it is only an administrative matter to find out where they can do it. It might be in the corner of a room, or in a corridor, or in the playground if it is warm. But the gains from tutoring are so considerable, particularly for the less-academically gifted children, that it seems even more important that they should have the chance to participate in it. Kids like Dave, Tony, Joachim and Neil are kids who stand to gain from tutoring. They are often kids who are not merely unqualified, but remedial, or backward, or whatever it's now called, themselves. But they are the ones who feel most deeply that school is a waste of time. And remember that the tutor gains most from tutoring, both socially and academically. If we give these kids the chance to be tutors learning will be painless and enjoyable for them. We are convinced that they would do it well. In fact, many of them would make better PE teachers, football coaches, art and craft teachers, than a good many primary school teachers. Why not let them try? The Haverstock School tutors brought primary children into their school to use specialist facilities like workshops and domestic science rooms. Why not?

But to undertake these schemes, schools have not just to make a few administrative shuffles. They have got to take a conscious philosophical decision. Decision made, the administration becomes slightly easier. Many teachers will no doubt heave a sigh of relief. No more of those inattentive early leavers, they're going to find out what hard jobs we've got. Now if the other arguments we have submitted failed to impress, this at least might make a mark. Much depends, of course, on the attitude of the 'receiving' teacher, in primary or secondary school, who is going to contribute by surrendering six or ten or twenty of his class to the tutors who arrive. They cannot exhibit 'professional' attitudes. Perhaps they will think of the pleasure they often find in teaching, and be prepared to share that. Again, tutors should be allowed to choose, as far as possible, what they want to do. And ideally the tutee would pick his or her own tutor.

We'd like to see schools make the decision to encourage tutoring by arranging their timetables to make it possible for all ages and abilities.

In Pocoma, California, an entire school has become involved in the development of a tutorial community project.... Presently grades 4–6 tutor students in grades K [kindergarten] – 3.

In Portland, Oregon, most of the children in high schools are engaged in an assisting programme....

... a more elaborate programme was established in a Detroit public school complex – a high school, a junior high school and an elementary school. Sixty-eight children participated. The older pupils met with the younger ones for a half hour a day, three or four times a week, helping in activities that ranged from drills on spelling words, maths tables and vocabulary, to making bookcases, sewing and publishing a class paper....[66]

The chain reaction, with students helping sixth formers, sixth formers helping the fourth year, the fourth year helping twelve year olds, who help tutor seven year olds, offers exciting possibilities. And then there are the real 'outsiders', mums who tutor in cookery, sewing, reading. Why not? Many primary schools do have mothers coming in to help with reading. And dad? Teachers are just not equipped to make some aspects of education more relevant, but the skills to complement their inadequacy are there in the community. If a school wants to run courses on decorating, or gardening, or car maintenance many dads could be course tutors.

A glorious cooperative picture is emerging: knowledge is shared, school buzzes with the community, children to and fro between them. Groups and pairs here and there are working together. It sounds a lot better than what we have at the moment.

8 Relevant Education

By now it should be clear. We are asking, explicitly and implicitly, for a change. A change in education. Changes in other community functions, which will be provoked by the change in education. Changes in other community functions which will become essential to the success of the change in education. A change to out-of-school education. A change to community education. Up to this point most of what we have said has been about practical methods of out-of-school education. In such practical 'de-schooled' education we see several values. First of all, it gives young people the chance to be accepted by themselves and their community as having a real function. They cease to be the mere recipients of education, youth services and general adult 'we know what's best for you' provisions; they learn by what they do and their self-esteem is increased by it. Secondly, this education gives an outlet to their energy and initiative, qualities which, at the moment, we paradoxically admire and repress. Thirdly, it makes learning 'for real', it offers kids an opportunity to develop their particular talents and their latent potential. Lastly, young people will be catalyzing the community to take over functions affecting the life of the community, functions which have previously been considered the province of a select group of professionals or citizens. Most important, they will be catalyzing the community to take over functions where professional or voluntary provision is failing. Already we have hinted at these failings. Now we examine some of them more carefully.

Education, the sort that goes on in schools and colleges, is clearly in need of some kind of a change. We, and many others, have no doubt about it. 'Why knock our education system? All kids go to school from five to sixteen. They don't have to pay for it, and British education – why, it's admired throughout the world. I don't know what you people want.' That's a regular answer to criticism of education in this country. It's quite valid. 'Schooling' has spread so rapidly that many people, today only middle-aged, were active in the fight for its growth. It is perfectly reasonable for them to object to people like ourselves who advocate change to a structure of which they are proud. But we suggest that it is no good to sit back too long admiring the edifice, we must probe and poke at it. It is far from perfect. This is because the institution, the idea of 'education' was not changed when it became universal and free. That very 'freeness' must lead to its modification, because education, if it is really to mean anything, must be all things to all men, rather than some pattern laid up in heaven which we can acquire if we have the inclination. In other words, though it may be a fine thing for all kids to go to school free, to many of them school is offering nothing besides inhibition and restriction. And the authority on which that claim is made is the authority of kids themselves. Wasn't there something once about education being a 'drawing out', a realizing of potential?

'School is a drag.'
'I can't wait to get out of here.'
'Nobody's going to tell me what to do when I get out of this place.'
'Stay on at school? – not likely, I want to do some living!'

In recent years there have been suggestions and demands for the destruction of existing educational structures and their replacement with new ones. Perhaps the most radical actual changes, as distinct from those which have been proposed and ignored, are exemplified by the free-school movement, young in this country, older in North America. The free-schoolers have created a smaller, non-disciplinarian environment for learning to take place, and learning takes place not only in that environment, but from it. We must take account of these qualities. But change in education has to go deeper than a few free schools in inner city areas, plus a few private experiments out in the country for middle-class fee-payers. In short, free school must not become a neat alternative for kids who can't cope with state schools in the cities and those rich enough to be able to buy their alternative elsewhere. For there are many kids who need a better education than is at present provided by the state. There will never be enough 'alternatives' for these children. And there is danger that the education establishment will be quite content with the odd alternative; too content to be radically affected by it. The majority of our children, academic and non-academic, are penned in institutions dedicated to competitive individualism, which completely fails those who are not academically inclined, and profoundly prejudices those who do succeed, by giving both an education that has nothing to do with real life. This education processes the successes for a place in the hierarchy of the Corporate State, while it relegates the failures to a space in the depths. Both failures and successes are unprepared for self-fulfillment. They are never excited into awareness, nor helped towards an active, questioning posture, confident to tackle the disorders and problems which affect their lives, as individuals and members of a community. A hierarchical, class-structured society must result from an education system which purposefully divides the winners from the losers. Of course, we can hardly throw out the 'academic' because of its harmful effect upon those unsuited to it. And it is unlikely that a change away from the 'academic' in our schools will lead to the decline in achievement of scientific research. But we must begin to soften the limited and narrow academic rod with which we break every child's back, with a little emotional, human learning. We need to cultivate people, and we won't do that by ignoring, throughout our education system, that the community, with all its problems, exists. We won't bring justice to the 46 per cent who leave school just as soon as they can by pouring in any amount of extra resources, teachers, modern buildings or by designating more and more priority areas. Education fails every child in every school simply because it has so little to do with his real life. It has nothing to do with his life because it has become yet another tool of the Corporate State. It is no longer the tool of the community.

The faults of the education system in Britain lie in two main directions: the content of education, and the structure of the system. These are interrelated issues, of course, and we have simplified the problem by dividing it into two like this, but this is supposed to be a simple book. The content of education includes the curriculum of each school subject, and those subjects themselves; it includes the way those subjects are communicated – the method; it includes the influences upon these two – children, or 'educators'. To separate these into separate items for analysis one by one smacks of the academic approach. Instead we will deal with them in muddled, and human, terms. We'll swallow them whole, if you like, rather than in tidy pieces. And some parts will be chewed over rather more than others. 'Structure' includes such subjects as the size of schools; what their function should be; whether they should even exist, or whether we should 'de-school' society, as Ivan Illich has it. Though 'structure' and 'content' are closely related, for convenience sake we will deal with content in this chapter and structure in the next.

'Service' is, at its best, a natural thing. One way to enable its natural occurrence is to encourage the utilization of individual skills and abilities in a social setting. But if 'service' is to be a part of our everyday lives, we must go further. The content of our education must become *relevant*.

Relevance means that our education must relate to our lives as they have been, as they are and as they will be. In that way those being educated feel that there is some *purpose* behind the process. But above all, it must have some purpose in itself. That is, we need to feel that in learning we are doing something useful. This reflects the point made at the beginning of the chapter. Young people need a function. Education has a duty to find and prepare them for that function, not to reduce them to bored, repressed and frustrated kids. That is relevance – learning, growing, developing confidence, understanding and personality, through doing something useful.

Increased relevance will not be brought about by trivial tinkerings with the school curriculum, tacking onto timetables something called 'social studies', 'social education', or 'community service'. Especially when it is only for the 'early-leavers'. Service has become something for the failures, emphasizing that they are failures, rather than something for all kids. okay – a dose for all kids, you may say. But that won't work either, for it will be an obvious appendage, as uninteresting and unimportant as Religious Education is to the non-religious, as craft is for those who always hit their thumb. Curriculum tinkering, humanities packages, moral education teaching material: none of it will help. Kids, immured in institutions transparently irrelevant to their own lives and their own needs, consider such material yet another facet of the great education confidence trick. And academics, despite curriculum developments of cataclysmic proportions, blithely follow their busy schedules, all unaware and unconcerned with any inadequacies in them.

What comes first – the community involvement or the education relevant to real individual and community needs? So far in Britain we have had some community involvement, either by the 'volunteers' or by the 'early leavers', but there has been no response from the 'content' of education. If community involvement does meet needs for many young people, then this will strike sparks from which, with a little pushing from the children, teachers can begin to relate their teaching. For example, if some children become deeply involved in work at a local mental hospital, teachers of varying subjects can begin to relate what they are teaching to the subject of mental handicap and illness. Art teachers on art as therapy; biology teachers on origins and treatments; physics teachers on electro-convulsive therapy; history teachers on Lunacy Acts, historical treatment and George III; English teachers with comprehensions describing handicaps and mental illness. Alternatively if this practical stimulus does not exist, and teachers have generally ignored it for quite a while as it is, then stimulus for practical action must come from a more relevant curriculum. And here we make no apologies for repeating our original statement: young people themselves will have to provoke this change to an education more relevant to their own needs. They must arouse themselves from the torpor induced by the education they have already had and say: 'Sir, is all this really helping us to understand the problems of society?' Or, as Charles Weingartner and Neil Postman put it in their book *Teaching as a Subversive Activity*, 'Sir that's crap!' Teachers who can take our criticisms of the 'profession' may start the change themselves. But they are part of the education system, and for every one concerned and enlightened teacher, there are nine or ten in the staff room, resisting change in their particular patch by every means that the 'professional' can muster. Children are not a part of the education system, and this is why it fails them. But as outsiders on the inside they are in an excellent position to do some changing. The system is meant to serve the children, and like all enlightened consumers they can vote with their mouths (crap) or with their feet (truant). Many are doing the latter, more can try the former.

We have said that schools fail. Many children find them unsatisfying, depressing, repressing, confusing, boring. There is failing number one. Children derive no benefit from school. They are neither prepared for life as a citizen nor, many of them, for the role designated for them by the Corporate State. So schools fail not only the community, but also the State. The State gets a bit agitated when it learns that reading standards have actually been declining in schools. So recent surveys announced, anyway. Putting aside the suspicion that the Corporate State might well be happy with illiterate workers, such surveys tell us that even faced with the simple task of teaching kids to read, schools fail. What's the solution? Unfortunately the immediate reaction is: 'more of the same'. Better trained teachers, more of them, more money – more provision, in short. This is a familiar escalation in every professional field. But it doesn't work. It's like the man with a headache: the doctor gives him codeine, it doesn't work. The doctor gives him more codeine: it doesn't work. Still more codeine, and it still doesn't work. Then the doctor realizes that the patient has a brain tumour. He takes it out. The man gets better. Operations are needed on education, too, not more financial codeine.

Then there's the problem of violence. The way the professionals dealt with this, when it came up yet again last year, was to talk about it, and inform a shocked population about it, in such a way that it appeared that 'violence in schools' was some sinister and evil characteristic of young people that teachers had to contend with. Fortunately, this coincided with a teachers' pay demand, and achieved even more publicity than it deserved because the major teaching unions disagreed on the facts and slanged one another about them. Rip-roaring stuff indeed! Actually the issue is not, surely, that teachers have to contend with violent young people; rather, *why* do teachers have to contend with violent young people? Why are young people violent? Repressed by schools, institutions, society, isn't this violence an expression of some frustration? Is tinkering with the curriculum and 'more of the same' going to satisfy a frustration verging on violence? Is it to school, and the education system as a whole, that we should look for answers? For one of the answers to violence will be more repression. Remember those boys from Brierley Street School, Crewe?

Then there's truancy. Here is a problem which the free-schoolers, at least, recognized as not being due to the inadequacies of children. It is caused by inadequacies of the schools that are meant to serve them, and patently don't. Teachers meanwhile are quite free to 'truant' from schools they don't like and seek employment elsewhere. Would they say that they themselves were to blame for this desire to leave, or the schools where they worked and were not happy? And is it mere coincidence that the school with a high teacher turnover, and a high supply-teacher rate is the school with a higher percentage of truants? Isn't it time we recognized that nobody is getting any pleasure out of that school? That school is the problem.

Besides these problems of 'education' there are faults which we have touched upon but which have been dealt with far more succintly by other writers on education like John Holt and Paul Goodman. There is the 'useless knowledge' syndrome, which means that teaching of material not only irrelevant to reality but irrelevant to anything. This material fills time. So when an extra year at school is foisted onto kids who want to drop out as soon as possible the amount of 'useless knowledge' they are in for is formidable. Then there is the 'narrow-minded people' syndrome. These are what schools produce. Some of them will be scientists who disregard the human problems which their training and intelligence might help to alleviate. And at the opposite extreme, most of them will be plain timid people who have no confidence in their own abilities and importance and do not realize that scientists, along with planners, sociologists, educationalists, doctors – all these professionals, in fact – are meant to serve them, not dominate them. These plain timid people do not realize that each one of them has more which is of value to the community than those professionals of whom they stand in awe, the sacred repositories of insight and knowledge. Hence these words from Jimmy Reid, Upper Clyde Shipbuilders' Shop Steward and Rector of Glasgow University, in his inaugural address:

I am convinced that the great mass of our people go through life without even a glimmer of what they could have contributed to their fellow human beings. This is a personal tragedy. It's a social crime. The flowering of each individual's personality and talents is the precondition of everyone's development.

In this book we have attributed this social crime largely to professionals who protect their own little area of operation. It must also be laid fairly and squarely at the door of an educational system which does little either to develop the contribution of the individual to the community or to encourage any contribution at all. It is all very well to concentrate on facts rather than emotion when educating, but it is failing to acknowledge that emotion is the very stuff of human interaction. Our children leave school immature in this direction. School structure and educational professionalism do not freely encourage outsiders into schools to present young people with alternatives for human interaction and emotional growth. At present this growth is limited to 'out-of-school' time, and it will continue to be so while schools will only welcome adults who have a teaching diploma to wave about.

We said that education should develop the contribution of the individual. This means that *what* is taught in school must be relevant to the lives of the children. At present it is concerned with their future jobs, and neglects the part of their lives which we will call their 'citizen life'. At a time when employment becomes scarce and leisure time greater, the only industry which is going to remain labour-intensive, non-mechanized, and non-technological in approach is the 'community industry'. This means people servicing other people. At the moment they don't service one another as much as they could, because they are not taught what to do nor how to do it. Also, to the layman, professionals have turned the 'community industry' into a technology itself. Community self-help is a part of out culture which is steadily being eroded. Schools need people-orientated education. People-orientated education is a way of preserving the best of

this culture, and a way of fighting the individualism that causes strife and inhumanity.

So schools must consider what they teach, and its relevance to the community. They must develop in each person the contributions which will enable interaction to occur, and in developing these, they must encourage the interaction itself. The latter means that schools must be pervaded by an atmosphere of cooperation, of willingness to serve one another. Because schools are dedicated to competition and training for 'success', they produce narrow-minded people.

This situation exists elsewhere. In our old colonies we imposed a similar educational system, on the same basis from which many now argue against change: 'It's the best system in the world.' So while our kids now bear the burden of the best system in the world, other kids bear a similar burden, many times magnified. The setting is different, the results even more horrific:

The education provided by the colonial government ... was not designed to prepare young people for the service of their own country;

instead it was motivated by a desire to inculcate the values of the colonial society and to train individuals for the service of the colonial state. In these countries the State interest in education therefore stemmed from the need for local clerks and junior officials. . . .[67]

President Nyerere of Tanzania, who wrote these words, may have felt that the colonial government was only perpetrating this non-community-oriented education in his own and other developing countries. But we have seen that the same thing was happening at home. For colonial government, colonial society and colonial state in the above, read Corporate State, and there you have 'developed' education in a 'developed' country.

Maybe that colonial education filled the bill in the pre-independence days. It was naturally available only to a limited number of children, otherwise there would be too many aspiring local clerks and junior officials! As the availability of education increased after independence in these countries, social and economic problems grew. To say that the social and economic consequences of a western education system in a developing country provided a mirror image of the situation in Britain today would be exaggerating. Parallels there are, it is true, but let us think of the image as one produced by the joke mirrors found in galleries at fairs and seaside piers. This misshapen image is worth examination, for it has one or two lessons for us.

Look at the winners and losers of our educational system. Finely equipped Corporate State winners, with their narrow-minded individualism and acedemic prowess, fit neatly into the higher echelons of a technological society and do not care about community life. Many will further the disintegration of the community by their own passivity or by the professional status which they hold as qualification to 'serve' the community. And then, in the blue corner, the hopeless loser, still with the narrow mind of the poor citizen, retaining the individualism inculcated at school, but lacking the academic prowess required for success, he fits neatly into the lower echelons of technological society. Losers care little for community life also, though often the communities in which they live have more of that life left in them than the communities of winners. Maybe losers still feel they need other people, unconsciously, while winners know they can make it on their own.

And their counterparts in the developing world? Joe was a loser, and a loser in a more highly competative academic rat-race than he would have found in Britain. But we must make one thing clear about Joe, even though it may sound obvious to any one who has experience in a developing country. Joe really wanted his education. Thoughts of dropping out as early as possible were far from his mind. Joe's aspirations, as a simple village boy, went further than the clerical/junior official level. Independence in his country meant that the whole white-collar range was open to him, and he wanted nothing less. There was nothing wrong with the aspiration, but the nature of the academic system, up which Joe has to make his way, left him nothing to fall back on should he fail. And Joe failed.

The end of the road came for him at O-level. Until then he had pursued a secondary course little different from that followed by boys and girls here. At O-level he failed every subject he sat, achieving the lowest possible grade in each. The fact that he did so unbelievably badly was the best of it. At least he knew that it was all up with him. Many students who only *just* failed went through a pointless succession of re-sits in a frantic attempt to scramble over this hurdle. As for Joe, his dream was shattered, but at least he could claim to have some education. However, the academic nature of it (he studied English literature, French, maths, physics, chemistry, biology and geography) meant that it was good for absolutely nothing. He still aspired to something, though, and who could blame him? But the irrelevance of this education to his own needs, and the needs of the village he lived in, made him ignorant. He had not even learnt anything about his vernacular language since his education had been conducted in English. So Joe's education had left him only one thing – pride. This pride kept him away from the community and culture of which he was ignorant. Yet opportunities for him away from that community were very few. In the end he was lucky to find a job as a primary school teacher far out in 'the bush'. Most young people in his position would drift to the cities and remain unemployed for a long time. Meanwhile their own culture and community needed them as people and contributors. But, with their heads full of French and physics, this is precisely what they were not. At A-level, at university entrance, at first- and second-year university exams, more Joes, or 'unemployed school leavers' as they are officially called, are produced. Going up the scale they have a little more academic knowledge, a little more aspiration to final success, a little less inclination to serve the community culture, and a little more ignorance of it.

Isaac, younger and cleverer than Joe, might well be a winner, though the hurdles are so high that he could stumble along the way and end up with Joe. But let us assume he graduates. The opportunities open are not vast, but there are few like him, so he won't have too much trouble finding employment unless, as has happened here, the unemployed graduate becomes an actuality. Isaac can, according to his desires, go in for white collar work in the government, into business, or perhaps continue studies with research at home or overseas. He may like to teach, and by doing so help his country by ousting an expensively paid expatriate. But in the city, he will probably tell you, 'What, me go to the bush – you must be joking!' The money Isaac is paid will go towards the physical symbols of success just as it will anywhere else. He'll buy a Peugeot or a Mercedes rather than a Rover, and very likely he'll become very much like his winning friends in this country, though his narrow-mindedness is probably not yet quite so extreme as theirs. He will still care for his relatives when they need his financial assistance. But there are Isaacs who will reject even that vestige of the extended family system. After all, you can't expect twelve years or more academic, competitive, individualistic, irrelevant education to leave much of a human being behind, can you?

Do we deny Isaac his success? Should his intelligence and industry go unrewarded? Of course not, and Joe neither. But what is the cost of it? Economically,

> It is now time that we looked again at the justification for a poor society like ours spending almost twenty per cent of its government revenues on providing education for its children and young people, and began to consider what that education should be doing. For in our circumstances it is impossible to devote Shs147,330,000 every year on education for some of our children (while others go without) unless its result has a proportionate relevance to the society we are trying to create.[68]

In the same way Britain should look again at our own £3 million education budget. And Britain is not the only country which should do so. But aside from economic considerations, since we have already voiced our distaste for talking cost-effectiveness and the like, there are far more important social considerations. Let us put Joe and Isaac into the broader context:

> the most central thing about the education we are at present providing is that it is basically an elitist education designed to meet the interests and needs of a very small proportion of those who enter the school system.[69]

That is true in Britain too, where 46 per cent drop out. President Nyerere means that only 13 per cent of primary school children make it to secondary school in Tanzania. For that 13 per cent,

> the education now provided is designed for the few who are intellectually stronger than their fellows; it induces among those who succeed a feeling of superiority and leaves the majority of the others hankering after something they will never obtain. . . . Tanzania's education is such as to divorce its participants from the society it is supposed to be preparing them for . . .[70]

Are these images of our own system so misshapen?

> . . .the vast majority [of our students] do not think of their knowledge or their strength as being related to the needs of the village community.[71]

That sounds like Jimmy Reid. For what is true of President Nyerere's villages in Tanzania and the young people who do not have anything to offer those village communities, is applicable to the less recognizable communities and the equally narrow-minded young products of schools in this country. The communities are less recognizable because they have been exposed to irrelevant education for far longer than Tanzania. And the difference between them is that Nyerere has had the vision and courage to do something about his irrelevant education system.

Throughout education the purveying of useless knowledge and the narrowing of minds continues. In institutions where courses for teaching diplomas and social-work diplomas are followed or in any place where 'career training' is offered, other forces are at work. For this is definitely training, not real education. Future professionals – teachers, social workers, doctors, policemen are trained to a dangerous point. It is a point where they learn little of the communities with which they will work. It is a training which prepares them to be not community servicers, but professionals enclosed in tight, compartmentalized, jargon-laden boxes; introverted, highly sensitive (to criticism from the non-professional), highly insensitive (to real human and social values). This introversion and reverence for their own professional status is encouraged by the training they receive. Above all, few are taught or encouraged to criticize the existing professional practice. That wouldn't do. This is a training process for the present system, so it is in current methods that training is given. Thus training for teachers takes for granted that the best way to educate young people is to enclose them in classrooms. Training for social workers takes for granted such sacred idiocies as the need for strict objectivity in casework. This means that rule number one for your social worker is: don't get personally involved. Such a rule might be sensible for doctors carrying out post-mortems, but . . .

The emotional involvement that there must be in teaching and social work is soon stifled by books like *Philosophy of Education*, *Sociology of Education*, *Educational Sociology*. (We have invented these titles, but they may well exist!) Let prospective teachers rather read George Dennison's *Lives of Children*. This is an emotional book about teaching kids. For that matter, let prospective social workers read it too, for George Dennison was a bit of both, and much else besides. That's an important point. Every teacher should be more than just a purveyor of knowledge. Purveying knowledge is a minor function. A teacher must be a social worker, a probation officer, a policeman (friendly variety), doctor . . . that'll do for a start. For only then can they educate children in their *lives*. The same applies to members of other professions. But we will stick with the teacher, for the narrow-mindedness which his training produces in him has odd results. Here is one. Schools are now beginning to appoint a teacher as a counsellor. That teacher is given training, of course. So all the other teachers, unless they are peculiarly thoughtful, consider that the new teacher/counsellor deals with the kids' emotional and social hang-ups. That leaves them freer for their real business – purveying knowledge. In Scotland a Green Paper recommended, among other things, the appointment of 'Assistant Headteachers (Guidance and Counselling)' not long ago. The mood of the profession can be judged by the immediate rush to carry out this recommendation. Assistant Headteachers (Guidance and Counselling) popped up everywhere. Need we say that every teacher should be a counsellor? Happily many teachers have already said it, themselves. The same situation arises over careers. Many schools appoint a 'careers teacher'. Why? Since, at the moment, the job a kid is going to get is an important part of his life, isn't it something on which the advice and help of all his teachers would be valuable?

So each professional box spawns smaller boxes. Such preoccupation with methods naturally obscures still further real thought about the result. And the result gets worse, not better. We have seen that there is an appalling lack of communication between the professions. The development of professions within professions heightens this. And meanwhile, back in the real world, people can't read, kids are fed up and violent, academics are more academic, scientists less human, and community life gets by as best it can on the undiluted paraquat provided by those wise and omnipotent professionals.

Results? Aside from teachers, what golden nuggets are the other professionals unearthing? Look at the mentally ill and handicapped. There are plenty of scandals here about violent treatment of patients, overuse of drugs and lack of real therapy. And the law-and-order professions? While there is considerable disagreement between the police profession and the legal profession over who is really innocent (or guilty), crime rates soar, juvenile delinquency is on the increase and drug-taking isn't really understood. The youth service? In spite of the numerous official reports produced about it, the youth service is just a joke, and rather a sick one. And in the field of medicine, the Christian Barnards pursue the frontiers of knowledge while increasing technology in medicine leaves millions without cure and care.

It's all a result of irrelevant education, whether academic, or 'training'. Are these people, from the Barnards, to the kid down the street, what we want and need? Are the professionals of our system really taking care of things properly? And by properly we don't mean economically and efficiently. We mean for the greatest good, for the greatest number, by labour-intensive methods and by making the utmost use of all skills, talents and social abilities available in the community. That isn't happening, the community stifles to death because nobody cares.

Any cynic will tell you that caring doesn't come naturally. All that stuff about Samaritans, that's a load of old rubbish. Darwin was right. The instinct for survival is too strong in us to permit the waste of time and energy involved in helping the less likely to survive. In fact this argument is so pessimistic it is almost too difficult to counter. We can only cite our own observations in reply. We have observed that it is not so: that people want to help but don't know how; that people want to be friends and don't know where to begin. So the cynic seizes upon ignorance and inability and makes a vice of them.

'Youth culture' gives us the clearest indications of a real wish to improve the human condition. Again open to criticism for conducting research in the wrong places we would point to that widespread phenomenon of youth culture – pop music.

'All the lonely people, where do they all come from?'[72] sang the Beatles, in a portrait of a lady totally unsympathetic, one would have thought, to most kids. Yet Eleanor Rigby wasn't a joke. 'He ain't heavy he's my brother.'[73] Yes, that is a line from a song, and the audience doesn't laugh at that one, either. It's a moving song, in fact, like 'Take a load off granny'.[74] The idea is that young bodies are better able to stand the strain than the disadvantaged. There is an acceptance of the different, and a strong commitment to peace, in much pop music. 'Let's make our world a good place for people to live in, so we can live in a world for which we care.'[75] That was a song with an 'environmental' slant. Then there's the one that says 'I believe, if you give a little bit of love to those you live with....'[76] You can't say it much more clearly than that. And nobody winces, or squirms and turns off the tranny, because at present the expression of such beliefs is neither embarrassing in style, or aimed at a cynical audience. It isn't by chance that this is a scene in which 'different' people flourish: an albino rock singer, a blind black man. Differences are acceptable for the variety and interest they bring. And for a long time now the very backbone of 'pop' has been 'the group', several people working together to make music. And though the money-making record business is the superficial forefront of the culture, its essence is the pop concert or the pop festival. Here the enjoyment of music is a communal thing, and one of the charms of the entertainment is that it's not so very hard to copy. Groups can be formed, singers imitated. The culture has its roots among the people still, and though the DJ might recommend this 'very professional' record, a whole lot of very amateurish stuff often becomes popular. At a concert the feeling is not of watching, but of participating. That was a feeling that attracted young people to the Proms, and it attracts them to pop festivals. The point of Woodstock was not the music, however exciting Santana and The Who can be. The point was 500,000 people living together for some days in peace and pleasure. Property shared, talking to the guy sitting next to you, helping the cold, wet and sick. After every similar festival in England the comments always refer to this communal spirit. Despite the commercial background these happenings have, the point remembered is that everyone joined in, helped out, loved. A guaranteed guillotine to this atmosphere would be its regimentation, the imposition of too much order upon it. The joy of it is chaos, spontaneity and participation. We have found that the performances at a festival, however fine, are subordinate to the event. And though the event seems to be yet another money-making gimmick, if enough participators arrive they can actually destroy organization and participate free! Government recommends: permanent sites with tents and toilets for future festivals. People warn: the more organization and facilities, the less kids will matter, the less they will want future festivals.

Certainly 'brotherhood' has gained amongst young people recently, often because it is such a rebellious cause! We refer frequently in this book to developments in the United States of America. This has led many to tell us that what happens there is not relevant here. But since we still tread the path towards the American Dream in Britain, but ten years or so behind in terms of material wealth to the individual, we consider it salutory to inspect the transatlantic scene and appreciate that this is the path we have chosen. Our goals are growth, materialism and mindless technology. And rebellion against these goals is 'brotherhood'. Brotherhood means that people are more important than money, big business, politics. Yet our schools, like our society, are dedicated to growth, materialism and mindless technology. And many young people, stuck in the established education system, are appalled at the strait-jacket in which they are trapped.

Essential to the acceptance of our suggestions is agreement that goals of peace, sharing and brotherhood are desirable. Suddenly we have people who do desire them. We have people who are ashamed because their countries oppress in their name, or cheat in their name, or kill in their name. Breasting the nationalist hill we find people on the other side. For this reason it is futile for our critics to claim that in citing Charles Reich or Ivan Illich we are referring to writers on an American situation. The situation we face has been created by the capitalist state, and we, and they, are concerned with the state of the people in this situation. Young people are disenchanted. This disenchantment was brought home to us strongly by two young 'successes'. The sons of a manual worker, whose formal education ended in his early teens, these kids have both survived the system to the higher academic reaches. They are called 'brilliant'. Both now want to 'drop out'. Unwilling to accept the roles they have learned – how to compete, acquire, within the system – they want to take manual jobs. They consider this a more honest course than to continue the academic careers open to them, because, as they told us, they didn't know anything at all.

So kids drop out. Sometimes they move about, hitching or biking to a more picaresque education. Again, once you accept that moving outside the confines of a school or a familiar society can be educative and can develop character, personality, confidence, then you admit the need for 'out-of-school' education. It might not be so ambitious as travel to Morocco or India, but it gives an opportunity for the young to encounter the unknown head-on. Such encounters are the very stuff of travelling, but they are available at quite a close radius from home. This is what we ask of education. That it permits young people to make these encounters and grow from them. If they learn nothing, their confidence will flourish.

But take a typical secondary comprehensive school today. How can you arrange an education system that enables young people to further their own commitment to brotherhood and change in society, enables them to go out, and see for themselves, starting from such a base? How fine if overnight the institution no longer existed! But we won't get that sort of revolution. So here are some suggestions for infiltrating the system as it is, exposing it to a little subversive activity, in order to condition it for later, more drastic, change.

Take the examination courses first. A-level. How on earth do you start humanizing A-level? Of course, nothing could be more inhuman than compelling a kid to fill sheets of paper for three hours in order to prove himself. But even an A-level course can be subverted. You're doing English Literature? We already mentioned Shakespeare. Nobody can deny the quality, profundity and value of the insights Shakespeare gives into the human condition. But they are insights of little value if not backed up by relevant experience, as many who understand Shakespeare would agree. What about the oppressed minority, in Shakespeare? Caliban might be the example. Or prejudice? Try Shylock, he will certainly illustrate the complictions of that particular human failing. Is Shylock relevant to *your* community? Or Lear's fool? Or any of those idiots who know so much? One of our own insights into the wisdom of Lear's fool was hearing a mad old lady wandering verbally and recognizing poetry, truth and relevance in her nonsense. That is just a recollection of our own. We are saying that the academic, laced with the community, constitutes a stronger dose than the academic taken neat.

Look at John Milton, for example, a stalwart of the literature syllabus. It might be a part of *Paradise Lost* the class is reading, perhaps two books of the twelve; or *Samson Agonistes*, or shorter poems. Even these most enthralled by A-level syllabuses would admit that detailed study of such minute portions of the man's opus is hardly a well-rounded introduction. So how about tackling the works of John Milton from a different angle? John Milton became blind when he was forty-four years old, as he worked hard on his reply to the European scholar Salmasius' attack on the Puritan government in England. Such a disability is so enormous, it cannot fail to influence every aspect of a man's life, especially if he is a poet. For Milton, as well as providing another of those ways of God to be justified to men, it gave a great extension of vision. No longer limited by the restricted world he saw about him, he could describe a hell beyond the sighted imagination, a place of size, colour and population too amazing for other artists to attempt. The disability drew him towards a blind hero Sámson, through whom he vented much of his own frustration at blindness, and who demonstrated that even the disabled could be of service. This feeling is expressed most directly in his *Ode on his Blindness*.

Now the key to Milton is not his blindness. That is merely a part of a whole. But it is a part that might be explored by schoolchildren, and might be explored particularly fruitfully with the help of a blind person invited to the class. And how interesting for that person, not necessarily an expert on Milton, to have the poet introduced and explained by the pupils, and then to discuss with them the parts of poems specifically dealing with blindness, or parts which seem to refer to it, or parts influenced by it. A valid consideration in this approach would be the classical attitudes to blindness so familiar to Milton himself. The master of the epic craft, legendary, blind Homer, produced the works used amongst the Greeks as the basis of education and religious training. There is little evidence with which we can substantiate Homer's blindness. We cannot even say when he lived, or whether he was one man or many. But the fact that blindness was ascribed to him tells us something of the Greek view of the disability. A man disabled in one direction was doubly able in another. He could not see things about him, but he could expatiate on invisible truths. There is the story of Teiresias, a common title for soothsayers throughout Greek legendary history, who was blinded by Athene but given inner sight as a compensation. Oedipus discovers truth and is blinded; as related by Milton the blinding of Samson leads to an inner strength that the minion of Delilah never possessed. And then there was Gloucester, who said 'I stumbled when I saw'. How does that compare with the way we consider and treat the blind today?

That's quite a learned way to consider blindness. Younger children are uninhibited enough to blindfold one another and assess the difficulties of negotiating the classroom, or even the streets outside. It's a good introduction for working with local blind children, helping them to gain confidence in the shops and streets of the town. Such a lesson with second formers might well be conducted by the sixth-former tutors who have just finished their English Literature lesson on Milton. Throughout the subject there are opportunities to introduce these 'angles' on novelist, dramatist, poet, which relate to modern social problems: Coleridge and drugs; Wordsworth and urban growth or The Idiot Boy; John Clare and gypsies; or institutions for the mentally handicapped, Dickens and .... The same 'angles' can be introduced in the study of French, German, Latin, Greek. Howard Moseley, of Eton College, prepared lessons for us on Greek and Roman attitudes to suicide. This could be studied by students following a classics course and reading the passages in the original, or students of general arts, social studies or religious education, who could read the passages in translation. Descriptions of the suicides of Phaedra and Ajax were recommended, with opinions on the subject from Plato and Aristotle. The Latin contribution included Virgil's description of the suicide of Dido, and Tacitus of the death on Seneca. The recommended discussion points are the motive for the act, the justification in each case and a consideration of others affected by it. In a modern context the class might consider the attitude of society today to suicide. What are the reasons for it, and how far do they resemble classical motives? What can we do today to prevent these causes? A visit from a representative of the local Samaritans is recommended as a suitable conclusion to the series of lessons, rooting them firmly in the practical present. It is hardly a revolutionary plan, yet here is a real attempt to tilt a study, often mocked for its irrelevance, in the directon of reality.

History lends itself particularly to this linking with the actual. The simplest link is the pointing of a contrast, for example, in the treatment of the mentally handicapped. This has always been part of the stuff of history classes, particularly in the lower regions of the school, but it tends to end with a pat on the back for the mid-twentieth century. Thank goodness, we say to ourselves, that we have a little more sensitivity than the voyeurs of Bedlam, as if putting out of sight and hearing were somehow better than gazing at them for our entertainment. There is a selfishness in both approaches which should disturb rather than lead to self-congratulation. After all, 'they' are in charge now, but are 'they' doing a good job? History lessons must sometimes show how little has changed. Were the enclosures of the Tudor period any different from compulsory purchases on proposed motorway routes?

To realize that people in the ssxteenth century felt equally helpless or hopeless in the face of the loss of their grazing rights, cottages and work, would help children to see that history is about people who, like us, had problems and feelings, while, at the same time, it would encourage them to think about some of the problems facing the society in which they live.[77]

Elsewhere we have described how a class used their art lessons to produce a mural for a playgroup. Extensions of this idea would include work in any institution to brighten up walls, tie-dye curtains, decorate screens. And naturally, work with patients on their own arts projects in mental hospitals, old peoples' homes.... In this subject there is tremendous scope for giving kids a 'real' job to do. Music, too, has a practical element which makes it easy to share. Michael Walker has suggested that a short performance by a trio or quartet might be taken to local hospitals or old peoples' homes. Since many school choirs sing carols at Christmas in local institutions, why not a group of harvest songs earlier, in the autumn term? Or Songs of Spring? Or a programme of Songs of the Sea, at other times? Mr Walker is full of such simple but lively suggestions. The basis of all of them is contact with the community through an academic discipline. And part of their essence must be that contributions from the community are welcomed. Here is another idea from Michael Walker, this time for C S E Music.

One suggestion for an individual project in music is the compiling of a concert programme. The student selects his theme, chooses his music; records can supplement his own performance and that of his friends; and he writes programme notes on the music and the composers. The programme ought to be performed – a lunchtime recital is often the answer, but time is short, and one feels that apart from the examination, the effort is out of proportion to the results.

Many hospitals have an internal radio system connected to earphones at the bedside. A programme of music, introduced with proper comments, could be prepared and recorded on tape. It could be enjoyable for the patients to hear and a very useful musical experience for the candidate. It would also certainly be more interesting to the Moderators than the duplicated sheets they sometimes see.[78]

The comment that in 'projects' the effort is out of proportion to the result, strikes home. Who hasn't worked with care and enthusiasm on some 'special project' which, handed to the examiner and assessed, becomes a pile of paper, however much time and effort went into its creation. And who hasn't looked at that pile of paper, even just a weekly essay, and thought – why? What was the point, really?

Our observations on music as a relevant study include the fact that Beethoven was deaf and Mozart a prodigy. And did you know that Elgar worked in a mental hospital for five years as a bandmaster, writing and arranging music for an assortment of instruments? Go along to your nearest mental hospital and find out what musical activities there are. Can you join in? Start some more? Start some?

And what about English Language? Some vocabulary lessons on the difference between spastic, mongol and autistic children might be useful. What is a neurotic? Or agoraphobia? Or alcoholism? Do class 2C know those long words? If not they've certainly seen a spastic and called him a 'nut-case'. And can class 3C fill in a form? They won't be much help to the old lady down their street if they can't help her with her forms. They might prove quite helpful to their own mothers, as well. Form-filling is a technique which all children need at some stage in their lives. And does class 3C know what to do if something they buy from a shop is defective? Or something their mum buys, or their old lady? Even A-level economics students know nothing about this real life problem at the moment:

The practice of forcing credit notes on to dissatisfied customers is wde-spread, but unjustifiable. The law is simple: if you return unsatisfactory goods, you have a right to damages under the Sale of Goods Act. These damages can be converted into getting a satisfactory replacement for the goods, or getting your money back. Any manager trying to fob you off with a credit note should be told that you will go to the County Court if not satisfied.[79]

But we must be careful not to give the impression that we merely propose the replacement of current subject curricula, composed as they are to a large extent of useless facts, with new curricula of facts slightly more relevant to real life. The central points may have become a little obscured amidst these ideas for re-orienting school curricula. Firstly, the curriculum must be a response to children's needs, a total response to their whole lives. Secondly, what is taught and the way it is taught must enable and encourage a questioning attitude, and questions must be pursued to their logical conclusion.

Here is an example of this. At the moment social studies courses in schools are likely to include a series of lessons about the welfare state. The teacher's knowledge is often hazy about the complexities of this subject, so he may invite outsiders to the school to talk about the topic. In two respects this is good thinking: the welfare state is important in our lives, so it is a good idea to find out about it; and it is good, too, that non-teachers have an opportunity to 'teach' in schools. But the exercise will lose its point if the questions are not asked, for only then will each pupil be enabled to assess the situation for himself. In other words, children must be allowed to have a go at these authority figures. The opportunity must be given for criticism. The kids might begin by asking: To the social worker: Could you please tell us how your training makes you more able to help a family in difficulties than anyone else, who is perhaps untrained, but wants to help? To the policeman: Do you know anything about the life-style and attitudes of the gypsies you keep moving on? To the housing/planning officer: Do you know or care that most people don't like high-rise flats? Do you know or care that property developers and middle-class people are buying up old houses round here and sending the prices sky-rocketing so that ordinary people haven't a hope of buying them? To the doctor: Why do you earn more money than my dad, who drives a train? Are you really worth so much? And so on. If the answers are evasive, then the very evasion will be on education.The authority figures will have revealed their clayfeet, and prove not so omnipotent as the children might have thought. They will come away with the feeling not that everything is taken care of, but that it is not. And they will wonder if there are not other ways of doing things. On the other hand, a rigorous and abrasive session with a class of kids will do the invited speakers a lot of good, and will provide them with more education than they've had for years. The question to be asked is, of course: 'What right have you, in looking after these things, to exclude us from having a go too?'

School and college courses in social studies, or sociology, or social science, have less and less to do with practical, emotional issues of life, and more and more to do with the theories of sociologists X, Y and Z. There are doubts about the necessity of a separate discipline at all. After all, we have been saying that every subject should be 'social'.

Let us explain some more conventional subjects to see how they can be given social purpose and meaning for young people.

Recently we have seen encouraging indications that geography is evolving more relevance to today's world. Waiting at the back of a class not long ago, however, we heard a fourth year learning about glaciers. Some, it appeared, flow faster than others. They flow out of cwms, over *roches moutonées*, and when they melt they leave moraines, and 'basket of eggs topography'. The teacher is working with this material either because it is on an exam board syllabus or, if the class is lucky enough to be without an exam board syllabus, because 'they have to be taught something, don't they?'

Of course the relevance or irrelevance of glaciers varies. Children in Wales may know a cwm, in Edinburgh they might live on a *roche moutonée*. But to the children we saw being taught about glaciers, there were geographical issues in abundance which had far more relevance to their lives. They lived in a new town. A teacher at a school in Stevenage realized that most of his children knew little about their town, and started a vigorous and imaginative inquiry by his pupils from a post mark on a letter he received. The postmark declared, boldly, 'Crawley – best of the new towns':

His class discussed this, and dispatched a letter to the local paper 'on behalf of the inhabitants of Stevenage' declaring the slogan to be 'distasteful'.

The newspaper seized the bait and sent a reporter to interview the class, with the result that the story got front-page coverage. (Headmaster objects? – better to warn him beforehand!) Earnest letters appeared next week from local councillors. A telephone call to the

BBC Radio programme 'South-East' brought further inquiries from Broadcasting House, and a radio discussion with the Town Clerk of Crawley and the Post Office.

An official from Crawley admitted that he considered the slogan an out-and-out gimmick. It was both good advertising and true, he claimed. 'If Stevenage objected to Crawley's claim their best move is to produce an even bigger and better story themselves.' So far as the Post Office is concerned, this kind of advertising is simply a source of revenue, but as the Stevenage paper commented, 'If the seaside resorts can come up with their sun-and-sands frankings, who is to stop us boasting of the joys of living in the Heart of Herts?'

The episode was followed by some comments in *Town and Country Planning* from Sir Frederic Osborn, father of the New Towns, who of course lives in Welwyn. He remarked about the postmark, '... I like this. I also like Stevenage's indignant protest and counter-claim. As to which is really the second-best new town – that is, best after Welwyn Garden City, I wouldn't have the nerve to pronounce. Nor which is the worst. Let us all cherish our superiority complexes and try to live up to them!'

Wise words. But the next step was that Crawley withdrew its postmark.

So far as Mr Wright's class was concerned the important thing the affair led to was a project on the comparative quality of Crawley and Stevenage, involving several disciplines: geology ('Crawley, on Wealden clay, tends towards a flat, uninteresting landscape, while Stevenage [on chalk and boulder clay] has a gently rolling landscape, providing an indisputable lead in architectural scope', etc.) geography of communications and map analysis, planning etc.

The story did not end there, because an article about the episode in the school magazine provoked further comment in the local press which provoked ... it almost goes on forever. And, remarks Mr Wright, 'Pupils *enjoy* it and feel *involved*!'[80]

Geography, as this shows, has been evolving into something of relevance, but we must just consider the examination argument. This says that while it is feasible to consider new and relevant studies for the 'non-academics', the academic types are held in a half-nelson by the examination syllabus. Glaciers, volcanoes, the distribution of turnips in Turkey and turkeys in the home counties, are *on* it, therefore they must be taught. Ingenious teachers can only make room here and there for relevant material. The fact that 'O' level courses shouldn't begin until age fifteen might tempt us to say that kids get a relevant education up to fourteen, and the non-academics thereafter. But that won't do, it merely tries to postpone the age of irrelevance from eleven to fifteen.

We subscribe to those ideas of Neil Postman and Charles Weingartner when they suggest that each child should nurture a built-in crap detector. This would enable them to say 'crap' to the teacher when he begins to tell them how glaciers in Greenland flow compared to those in Switzerland. Teachers needn't feel too smashed by this reaction. They should just pass the message up to the exam bodies, with a suitable expletive as accompaniment. But already they have some areas for encouragement and growth. Many readers may not know that there are syllabuses in the Certificate of Secondary Education known as Mode Two, and Mode Three. In these no course is prescribed. Teachers make up courses for their own kids, and the results are submitted for external marking, or marked by the teachers themselves.

But why the hell have exams and syllabuses anyway? Syllabuses mean learning for the sake of learning rather than for its value to the lives of people. But while suggestions about the modification of syllabuses are minor and conservative compared with the changes we should like to see in educational structures, they are worthwhile if the questioning of content and relevance leads kids and teachers to question the existence of the syllabus itself. What is this plastic container in which 'education' is purveyed? It may seem indestructible but you can melt holes in plastic quite easily. The first assault might come from Mode Three. Kids and teachers together decide a course: easy for CSE, not for GCE. But in the latter new syllabuses can be drawn up. A group of teachers in Hertfordshire produced one for A-level environmental studies not long ago. But how can syllabuses be changed? Here group effort is essential. Sadly, teaching unions spend much of their time mixing talk of salaries and professional status with moaning and groaning about issues which they feel are beyond their control. This is a pity, for these are groups with potential to change, for they could say a loud 'Boo' to the examinations boards. In saying it they would be responding to the needs of children and to the needs of community life. If they, through that 'Boo', were to opt out of processing children for higher education and business and to opt into 'real' education, it would be a brave step.

That is hardly a question for the geography lesson. We do not suggest that all geography be based on a child's local environment and local environmental issues. But a large part of it should be, for this is where most of them will live for most of their lives. Such environmental education is the core of the new geography and is taking in many other subject areas. We have already looked at the kinds of practical work in the environment which can emanate from the contribution to such environmental education without saying what we mean by environmental education. It is not one step forward from geography, but two. The first step was environmental studies, and rural studies. These disciplines say, 'Don't learn about the environment in the classroom, learn in the environment.' That is sensible. There would have been more point to those glaciers if the kids could have seen one. But environmental education took the next step. 'No good learning in the environment unless one encourages a sense of real concern', say the environmental educators. Concern is the precursor of change. One environmental educator was Christopher Searle, an English teacher. Seeing the local environment as a stimulant to creative writing, he encouraged his kids in a Stepney school to look at their environment and say, in poetry, what they thought of it. He responded to their needs, and he got sacked for it. For he published the poems, without the permission of the school governors and, worse still, many of them painted embarrassingly clear pictures of Stepney: drab, filthy and run-down. Searle was sacked. Local headteachers banded together to prevent him from teaching the children he dearly wanted to teach. And whose needs were the governors and headteachers responding to? The whole business was dangerous for them. The children might begin to suggest what the environment should be like, and that wouldn't do.

Where the geography teacher teaches his class about industry on the River Weaver, the environmental studies teacher would take his kids there. The environmental educator would do that too, and then he would get them to find out how each industry contributed to pollution of the river and how such pollution compared with, say, the Rhine in Germany, and the Seine in

France, and the Amazon and Orinoco. But local issues are the important ones:

It is easy to forget, in this age of motor cars, that a town or city is made for people and not machines. Although we may bemoan the fact that cars are destroying the urban environment, nevertheless one of the commonest kinds of urban studies carried out as educational fieldwork is to make traffic surveys. Fair enough in certain circumstances perhaps, but on the whole such investigations are more likely to be done as exercises in simple statistics rather than as an inquiry into the urgent problem of the pedestrian/traffic conflict occurring daily in our towns . . .[81]

It goes without saying that the move from statistical exercises to involvement in a complex issue affecting local people is the essence of environmental education and 'real' geography. Keith Wheeler, in the article from which we quote above, suggests seventeen different ways in which children could look at the people-versus-cars issue, over pedestrianization alone. They include collecting newspaper cuttings about road accidents to pedestrians pin-pointing risk areas; interviewing people to find out if they would like streets turned into pedestrian precincts; drawing up a local pedestrians, 'Bill of Rights'; teaching road safety to younger kids; calculating 'Pedestrian Amenity Indexes'; mapping pedestrian flows; acting out the plight of an elderly person trying to cross a busy road. These are just a few of his ideas. But what sort of trouble are kids and teachers going to find themselves in if they stir up a local controversy over pedestrianization? Will their fate resemble Chris Searle's?

Pedestrianization is one example. In environmental education key community issues must find a place: slum housing, lack of open spaces or play facilities, motorway developments and high-rise dwellings. We will continue to live with the inadequacies of professional planning until we educate our young to realize that it is the wishes of people that matter, not the whims of professionals.

Other subjects make their contribution also. Every 'A' level chemistry student can tell you about cyanide, sulphur dioxide and the structure of polythene. How many know anything about cyanide disposal, atmospheric pollution by acids, or the 'non-biodegradability' of plastic. (Wow! – it means that every plastic bag we use is here to stay, there is no way of returning it to a place in the natural order of things. No way.) Students don't know about these aspects of chemistry for they are educated by non-environmental, irrelevant processes. Monitoring teams will only be formed by the stimulus of real science, not from the nonsense contained in most science syllabuses.

Isn't it wasteful to have professional teachers giving lessons on India and Pakistan? These lessons concentrate on facts and figures about jute, tea and the Indus and ignore the presence in the local community and the school itself, of people who were born in India and Pakistan. Crises such as the war in Bangladesh deserve the wholesale suspension of lessons on glaciers and volcanoes in favour of detailed study of the problems involved. And the latest council plan to build on the only local open space deserves the same treatment.

Meanwhile, back in the biology lab, bean shoots are growing and dog-fish being dissected. Nobody talks about the causes and effects of arthritis, the causes of mental handicap, the effect of artificial weedkillers on birdlife, the effects of lead on the human body. Psychological illnesses are not discussed. At the same time as physics students study the radioactive elements and their properties, another hydrogen bomb is tested in the Pacific. What effects is that going to have? In maths, sets and statistics are learned as if they didn't exist in the local community. In geology Cambrian and Ordovician stratigraphy is studied while Rio Tinto Zinc carve cambrian and ordovician rocks out of gargantuan holes in Snowdonia. In home economics, meals are cooked while old folk in the town fight to make ends meet.

Elsewhere, pharmacy students learn about the chemistry of drugs, not the psychology of addicts. Design students make expensive furniture for the benefit of Sunday supplements while a handicapped person wonders how to make it upstairs. Architecture students design bachelor flats while Shelter tries to find housing for the homeless. Law students learn by heart Rex versus Smith while Mrs Smith has a nervous breakdown trying to exist with her kids while dad is away.

In earlier chapters we described the scope for practical relation of subjects to the provision of services for the community. We believe that every subject must become relevant to this function whether in theory or practice, if the community is to be revitalized. In short, subjects like history, literature and languages provide opportunities, and not just in local terms. It is vital to investigate local history, using old people as resources; it is vital to act on local environmental issues; and it is vital to study the languages which local immigrants have brought with them to our cities. But history and literature also provide a perspective. We might, for example, compare our own treatment of gypsies with the way they were treated in Tudor or Victorian times. Yes, it does mean a lot of work for the teacher, but such perspectives can enable children to consider alternatives, can enable them to question and perhaps to see limitations to attitudes they have taken for granted. Geography likewise. Why learn that cocoa comes from Ghana and not bother to learn something of the cocoa farmer's community? Does that community have anything to teach us? How do people live? Languages are indispensable in this type of study. Students of Russia might try translating bits from *Pravda* about collective farms rather than passages from set books. And does economics have to be concerned with figures and statistics? What about *people* who are unemployed? They are referred to by the economist as 'unemployment'. What happens to people in slumps, overproduction, gluts? Shopkeepers and employers might give kids some insight into how these things happen on a local level. And in the sciences let us see more relevance in the manner of Mrs Barrett, at Walkden School, Manchester. The aim must be the use of science and technology by the local community, and a human perspective for those who will be professional scientists. In Leicester, in response to a request from an educational psychologist, a school electronics department produced a device to provide audio-stimuli for work with autistic children. That is the sort of exercise we applaud. The less all this learning takes place in the classroom, the better. The classroom is separated from the realities of social and physical environment. True relevance can best be achieved 'on the spot'.

There are people who say, 'That's all very well, but what about the basic skills – reading, for example.' It's all a question of motivation. If what is learnt excites and challenges a young person, then he will seek to learn, even basic skills. Now the excitement and challenge has to be offered by the purpose of the learning, rather than by some inherent excitement in the subject itself. We have seen that only a minority of young people can respond to the latter. We are suggesting that the purpose of re-activating communities offers challenge and excitement. A young person might be motivated to learn to read because he wants to understand the plans for the adventure playground, or the questionnaire on locating a hostel for handicapped adolescents in the community. And it is not just community issues which provide this stimulus. The remedial reader is more likely to turn on to old football programmes and magazines than first-year readers. To those who scoff at this as wishful thinking, remember that Paulo Freire, working in Brazil, found poor illiterates able to read those words which mattered to their lives before any others. And volunteers working with gypsies have found them much keener to learn about carburettors and pistons than John and Jane stories.

These are ideas which seem to us to illustrate a way of re-orienting the content of education. We have given only tiny examples in this chapter, not a comprehensive programme. Every school will make its own programme according to the needs of its community. But it's time the world of educationists and teachers stopped to consider whether there might be a point in incorporating some of what we suggest into curricula now. Education is not geared to the production of citizens who understand themselves as part of a community of people. If they have this understanding, might they not prove active, change-seeking, questioning, caring people? Who is it who is afraid of this possibility? Education is increasingly machine-oriented, because society is increasingly machine-oriented. Education is wasteful of 'human talent'. Because society is wasteful too. Education and its irrelevance is a tool of the Corporate State. About time we had some real education, for a change.

Which brings us back to Tanzania again. We described the problem earlier; now a brief look at the suggested solution.

> It would be a gross misinterpretation of our needs to suggest that the educational system should be designed to produce robots who work hard but never question what the leaders in government or TANU are doing or saying. For the people are, and must be, government and

TANU. Our government and our party must always be responsible to the people, and must always consist of representatives – spokesmen and servants of the people. The education provided must therefore encourage the development in each citizen of three things: an inquiring mind; an ability to learn from what others do, and reject or adapt it to his own needs; and a basic confidence in his own position as a free and equal member of the society, who values others and is valued by them, for what he does and not for what he obtains.[82]

These three objectives are a good start towards a solution:

Most important of all is that we should change the things we demand of our schools. We should not determine the type of things children are taught in primary schools by the things a doctor, engineer, teacher, economist or administrator should know. Most of our pupils will never be any of these things. We should determine the type of things taught in primary schools by the things which the boy or girl ought to know – that is the skills he ought to acquire and the values he ought to cherish if he or she, is to live happily and well in a socialist and predominantly rural society, and contribute to the improvement of life there.[83]

Again, with the alteration of a few words, the thinking is applicable to education in Britain. In Tanzania the emphasis is on primary education since most pupils cannot continue beyond this. But Tanzania's primary leavers are similar to our 'early leavers'.

Our sights must be on the majority; it is they we must be aiming at in determining the curriculum and syllabus. The purpose is to provide a different education – one realistically designed to fulfil the common purposes of education in the particular society of Tanzania. The same thing must be true at post-primary schools. The object of the teaching must be the provision of knowledge, skills and attitudes which will serve the student when he or she lives and works in a developing and changing socialist state; it must not be aimed at university entrance.[84]

For 'post-primary' read 'academic'. It is not 'we' who must determine the curriculum and syllabus in Britain, it is kids. Nyerere's authoritative 'that is what we will give our children' is not out of place in his situtaion. He is making a national declaration of intent, after all. In this book we are creeping in the back way with subversive methods attractive to the enslaved rather than the authorities.

As one of his recommendations for more relevant education in Tanzania, President Nyerere proposes that schools have their own farms. These would not be mechanized showpieces but labour-intensive, learning-on-the-job resource centres. Through the school farm students would learn the advantages of co-operative endeavour, and that their standard of living would depend upon their efforts on the farm. No work, no grub, in short. Can we not apply this idea here? Instead of their farm, children have their community, which similarly depends on their efforts? Nyerere says: Look, we've got an agricultural economy and a culture which we should be proud to keep and remember, so there's no point in destroying the latter, and setting the ambitions of our pupils far above the former; our education must be relevant to the one and take full account of the other.

Now there is our own culture and heritage. Within it communities did once exist with more interaction and cooperation than they can boast today. The professionals who oversee our welfare may be handy, but they must be our servants, not the masters they have become. And education must be a preparation for life, not university entrance or dropping out. We have poured scorn on economy and efficiency, but it may be these which ironically provide the impetus for the change we advocate. As our technological society increasingly renders people redundant, they will be able to work only in the one field which is not organized, mechanized and computerized: the people business. This business must stay as people-oriented as possible. In schools kids must be prepared for that business, prepared to criticize and change it. And they must be prepared to care for one another within it, to respect and value one another within it, and to make of it a more vibrant and living thing than any organized and mechanized business. Then the real changes will begin in earnest.

None of this will be achieved by pathetic tinkering with the present system. At the moment education is a system switched permanently to 'on' with the 'off' switch out of sight and reach. We can top up the oil, adjust the carburettor, fill up the radiator, even adjust the tappets for a sweeter tuning. We can pour in thousands of pounds for curriculum development, more teachers, better buildings, better equipment. The image is more glossy but the product is as lousy as it always was.

The first task is to find the 'off' switch and, in the ensuing peace, ask whether the machine should be scrapped wholesale. Which market is the product aimed at anyhow? If we decide that the new market is the community, then we can start re-designing the machine. We propose in the next chapter more, smaller versions, to replace the monsters we had before. All will have 'off' switches bigger than the very machines themselves. We don't want to make the same mistakes again.

9 Relevant School Structures

But can the school ever be the focus of community life we have described if it has the structure of a contemporary school in an urban area? It is hard to imagine. And can the content of education ever be made properly relevant in schools as they exist in Britain today? Schools will only be related to communities when schools, are part of communities. Yet gigantic comprehensive schools grammar schools and public schools do not meet this simple criterion. They are not part of the community because many of the children who attend them travel away from their own communities to attend school. On the other hand, primary schools have far more chance to become 'community schools'. Often secondary modern schools have a chance, too. Small comprehensives likewise. In rural areas the village colleges of Cambridgeshire are a clear attempt to avoid a familiar pattern. Country pupils often travel a long way to attend school.

At the age of eleven many boys and girls leave their local primary school to begin an irrelevant education in an institution some miles from home. An irrelevant education in an irrelevant situation. It seems that nobody stopped to wonder if large, non-community-based schools with large catchment areas were right. Economy rules education, and economically speaking it was quite sensible to group pupils of an academic inclination into a unit serving more than one community. Hence the university, the sixth-form college, the grammar school. For every community secondary school can't have elaborate science labs and art equipment, language laboratories and all that paraphernalia. There aren't enough maths teachers to go round, so they are concentrated in larger schools and so on. There are all kinds of reasons for non-community schools, many of them economic. Too many of them. There are not many *social* reasons for non-community schools. We cannot think of any, actually. But there are plenty of social reasons against schools structured in this way. Clearly they have no proper roots, they do not belong anywhere, only in the education system. The best they can hope for in terms of identity, is to resemble other non-community-based schools. Not for them the singularity of belonging to this place or that, this end of town or the other. The form of the school also makes it difficult for the people who live near it to feel involved in it: it is often a large impersonal unit, daunting and unfriendly to the outsider, and the insider too.

Two thousand-strong comprehensives are education gone mad. 'Comprehensive' is Book One in any sane scheme for relevant education. Of course children of differing abilities and potential must be together for one of the most elementary forms of interaction to take place. There is no longer any debate about that, surely. But two thousand – that's an awful lot of kids. And the 'purpose-built' school – it may look very nice, but behind the glossy façade, pleasing to politicians and local councillors, behind the expensive facilities, there is yet another impersonal machine. Powered by streams, of course.

Because the debate over comprehensive education seems to us a historical one, we will only mention here that many comprehensives seem to be secondary modern and grammar schools contained in one building. It is not our purpose to evaluate the various systems that local eductaion authorities operate, or try to operate. But we have to point out that practical community action and an education relevant to it, backing up and following up, will be effective in schools which have definite roots in the area round their buildings. Can we excite children about local problems in a place which is not their locality? Are their parents going to become involved with them, if it means travelling ten miles to the school? Surely the whole point of the education we are recommending is that its resources exist in our immediate environs, as part of our everyday, out-of-school life. Our in-school life must learn to draw on these same resources. Therefore our schools must be in the same environs as our homes.

But while it is one thing to effect changes on the content of education, and children and teachers can both be agents of this change, altering the structure of schools is an altogether tougher proposition. Schools, especially large ones, represent enormous financial investment. It may be an attractive idea to blow up a large, purpose-built comprehensive, but it isn't very practical. So we are caught again in the old economic arguments. The smaller the school, we are told, the greater the per capita cost of education for each child. Education is expensive enough, so keep costs to a minimum by building large units. So goes the thinking. The thinking implies that what happens to the children is of secondary importance. And what happens to the communities in which they live is an even lower priority. So the structure of schools is governed by financial considerations, not human ones.

Schools must be small. They must be small enough for some 'group identity' to exist among the teachers and pupils. Such group identity doesn't even exist among staff alone in large schools. More importantly, schools must be small enough to be an acceptable and indistinguishable part of a community, which people from the community can enter without the timidity induced by 'purpose-built' institutions. Schools must be small enough for teachers to become involved with children, for children to become involved with the community, for the people of the community to feel that the school is 'their' school, not 'a' school. Such a school will not have or need the facilities of a large school unit. Its resources will not be language labs, or modern science equipment. These resources are lost to young people the minute they leave school, anyway. But the resource of the community school will be the community, in two ways. The school will enable children to learn about the community in the community. 'Lessons', if they can be called that, will take place in the hospital, in the playgroup, with immigrant families, and so on. The educational methods (since everybody cares so much about method in the educational world) in these situations are: involvement as opposed to mere observation, and questioning, rather than tacit acceptance. The involvement gives young people an active function in society. The questioning will lead to continual change, continual reappraisal of methods and structures which too often at present are rigid and ossified.

Secondly, just as young people will learn in the community,

and have free access to the places and people they can serve, learn about and question, so the community must have a free access to the school. A sign over the door saying 'All welcome' won't do, for just as young people must have a function in the community, so the community must have a function in the school. This is not just the function of concerned parents, trying to find out how young Tom is doing, either. That is a passive function. If the education in a community school is going to relate to both the community and the individual needs of young people, there will be many people in the community who can relate it far better than many conventional teachers. Earlier we mentioned that doctors, policemen and social workers might come into a school to tell young people what they do and, perhaps, to be influenced by critical questioning from their audience. Now we must take this thinking further, for there will be many who can teach what they know, or what they do, in the same way.

Look at some topics close to the 'community issue'. The best way to enable learning about handicap to occur is, of course, by enabling children to work with handicapped people. Earlier we suggested some practical ways that this could happen. Reciprocally, a classroom lesson might also prove useful. Teacher is in a wheelchair, responding to questions which will help the class to understand important aspects of handicap: 'Were you handicapped from birth, or by an accident?' 'What's the difference between a para-plegic and a tetra-plegic?' 'What kind of benefits do you get from the State?' 'What kind of work can you do?' 'Will you be able to have children?' 'Will the baby be handicapped?' 'Would you prefer to live in a home with other handicapped people, or as an ordinary member of the community in your own place?' 'What kind of things are you good at?' There are many more questions, some considerably more down to earth than these. The presence of a handicapped person may well be desirable in a variety of classroom settings. A technology lesson considering wheelchair design would be incomplete without such an expert, a biology lesson on the causes of handicap likewise. We have already suggested a blind teacher in a lesson on Milton; how can games and exercises suitable for particular kinds of handicapped people, from arthritics to tetra-plegics, be devised without the expert advice of the handicapped themselves? If a school regards learning about handicap as important – and surely it is, if present prejudice, inhibition and ignorance is to be overcome – then the resource is human.

The same applies in other fields. If a school is situated in an area where there are citizens from other countries (immigrants if you must), then it surely goes without saying that there must be an educational response to their presence. And there is no better way to find out about the history, geography and culture of India, Pakistan, St Kitts, Greece, Cyprus, Italy, East Africa or wherever, than by learning about it from the Indian, Pakistani, *et al.* He may be a bus driver, but the school needs him as a teacher. His qualification is his willingness to help out. The immigrant children in the school will assist the process, but their parents will know more, and have more experience to answer the questions of a class: 'What did you do for a living in India?' 'Exactly where did you live? Show us on this map!' 'What was the climate like?' 'Why did you come here?' 'Do you ever want to go home?' 'Is your hair curly, like West Indians'?' 'Why do you cover your hair with a cloth?' 'Why is it called a turban?' 'What's special about your religion?' 'How come you're Indian, yet you lived in East Africa?'

As with the handicapped, 'expert' lessons like these will lead to, or follow from, practical community service work. According to the age of the class the questions might be more or less complex. With the bus conductor, for example, discussion might bring home to the kids that there is prejudice in the fields of jobs and housing. If estate agents and employers are discriminating against black people, what is the school going to do? Perhaps they could really get moving, accompanying black people to interviews, and probing house agents? They may find that writing to the Race Relations Board or the Community Relations Commission is no more effective than contacting the Alkali Inspectorate over air pollution. What matters is what the community schools of Sparkbrook and Southall are doing about the prejudice in their communities.

Then there's food. Who eats what, and how do they cook it? Most home economics teachers are ignorant of the secrets behind chapattis, papadoms and curry. Perhaps the bus driver's wife would help? Then there's language. Is it just for kids to help immigrants by tutoring English? Couldn't they have a go themselves at Hindi, or the Kingston version of the Queen's English. That seems to be having a pretty strong effect on young language anyway. So maybe it's as relevant as French and German?

This notion of people, the community itself, as a resource, is more than an additional means towards understanding of community problems. Perhaps the wheelchair teacher speaks French, or is an expert model maker, or bee keeper? As Jimmy Reid said, 'a great mass of people who go through life without even a glimmer of what they could have contributed to their fellow human beings.' Paul Goodman calls school a 'pitiful waste of youthful years'. Would those youthful years be quite so wasted if kids learnt real things from real people, themselves wasted at present? The social equation sounds simple. It is.

At the moment A-level students of politics and economics, and university students likewise, study trades unions without ever meeting a shop steward. There are likely to be shop stewards in most communities, to say nothing of the old people who were out of work in the 1930s, or the ordinary people whose jobs are threatened by mechanization, asset stripping and redundancy today. Will human values, rather than economic values ever, seep into schools, when businessmen of future years are not learning that the Jimmy Reids are not 'Reds', but people who care about the lives and livelihood of their fellows? Of course, if all knowledge comes from teacher and the book, it is hard to appreciate that the best way to understand the union movement is to talk to some members.

And isn't it a pity, in these days of easy travel, that kids in school and college can learn about things or people, without ever seeing the things or meeting the people? Geography field trips and 'work experience' are usually inadequate. The former should involve children in some other community, for a period of time. At the moment it is merely a series of 'on location' lectures. Thus a party of kids from an urban area might sample commuter land, and vice versa, both in the 'real' sense. This would seem more interesting and useful than coach trips and note-taking. The questioning approach must again be adopted. The community, like anything else, in spite of the stimulating work done by young people, may well become run down. Active, lively, questioning visitors will see the community as something new and may produce ideas, and ask the 'wrong' questions. This will be another stimulus.

Such interchanges are primarily valuable as a way of understanding other things, other people outside the local community. When the job is 'the thing' one can only really find out about it by doing it. So work experience is valuable. Over-the-shoulder work experience isn't. Community service often overlaps with this at the moment. Kids might be working in a hospital not so much to help others but to help themselves to discover whether such a career takes their fancy. But you're not going to find out much about nursing if you're only allowed to take round the tea and arrange the flowers, are you? When we described this work earlier we pointed out that it helped neither the young person, nor the hospital. Similarly work-experience ventures in factories, offices, often lapse into the same over-the-shoulder pattern. Always one step back from real experience, real responsibility. More realistic is the approach mooted by the education authority in Fife: a factory producing goods for sale, particularly goods which schools need. The workers? – kids, of course.

But returning to our immigrant for a minute, let us remember that he has not only a culture to contribute. He is a bus driver too, and may be a stamp collector. So he can help the class find out about his job, and share his interest with younger enthusiasts. A skill is a key to entry into an institution. The model for the operation is entry into the school. The community will enter if it has a function. That function must be to help kids by passing on and sharing skills. Cliff Edwards' barrow-boy English tutor had a skill. He could read. Most people can read, so they are in a good position to help kids do the same. And it is clear that in the community ventures we have described, young people will need to call upon the skills of adults. Electricians, plumbers, builders, lawyers, accountants, engineers – all will have a place in the school, for they will be needed by young people for themselves and for their skills. They know things kids need to learn, and these things will be learnt best at first hand, rather than via the teacher. And kids will need the practical help of skilled adults: the lawyer in the gypsy case, the electrician with the wiring of the old folks, emergency alarm devised in science class, and so on.

The participation of adults does not only supplement the efforts of kids in community ventures, nor does it only give kids more resources for learning. It means that the whole community movement will be a joint movement, rather than a young people's movement. Just as kids suspect and despise the way adults use 'power', so adults are liable to feel left out and suspicious of any phenomenon which seems to them to be exclusively youthful. But if it includes them from the very beginning, then they may find a chance for fulfilment in it also. For it is not just young people who have trouble communicating with adults. There are definite difficulties of vocabulary and thought in the other direction also. Working together in a cooperative project for other people is a good situation for interaction to occur. And since it is not just young people, but most people, whose talents are wasted, all people must therefore have an opportunity of working together and learning from one another.

So all a school really needs is to be small, in the community (any old house will do), without too much in the way of books, science labs, language laboratories, 'resource centres', ed-tech equipment, administrative headmasters and other educational embellishments. Then the community must question the content of the school curriculum and the validity of the subjects in it. Having sorted that out, they look for human resources. Perhaps these will be older students in the school, who act as tutors, as college students. Then these people will have a function. And learning will be humanized a little. Language labs are nothing to be proud of; like machines to teach maths, reading and spoken English, they are anti-people, when there are plenty of people on the school's doorstep capable of teaching things. Nowadays children associate 'science' with 'laboratory' and with equipment of ever increasing complexity, like ripple tanks and other Nuffield-inspired junk. Science is no longer about the air we breathe, the water that comes from the sky, the insects, animals and birds that live around us, the light we see by, the products we manufacture and the resources we destroy. To young people science is about ripple-tanks, accumulators, diodes, burettes, concentrated sulphuric acid and iron filings. They notice only cursory references to the relation of science and their lives.

The school laboratory, along with all the ed-tech hardware like PE equipment, stage and drama gear, wood and metal-workshops, is useful and valuable to only a small percentage of the children in the school. All will learn, however, that 'drama' is what happens on the school stage; that 'language' is learned from a machine; that 'science' equals bunsen burners and test tubes in the lab. None of these elaborate and expensive resources serve the community, few of them serve all the children, all the time, and all of them will be unavailable to the schoolchild when he leaves the school for the community. Our culture and community does need some scientists, dramatists and linguists, so we must admit the need for elaborate equipment at some stage or other. But these will be the few, and that equipment is not necessary in every school because it is not relevant to most children. And young people should not approach it until they are fully convinced that science can be learnt from the environment, that language is spoken by people, and that drama and art can exist off the school stage and outside the art-room, on streets and walls. In short, ed-tech runs amok, just as management consultancy does in business.

School buildings themselves are underutilized. That is already widely recognized. Why invest hundreds of thousands of pounds on building a school when the buildings are used for, at the most, thirty-six five-day weeks from nine till five? Quick mathematics will tell you that this means the buildings are being used only 50 per cent of the whole year. Now as long ago as 1964 the Department of Education and Science issued Circular 11/64 to local education authorities. This dealt with the under-utilization of sports facilities, and advised that schools should let the general public have access to playing fields, etc. Six years later Circular 2/70 recommended that the same thinking should be applied to 'school facilities'. A quick check on your local school will probably reveal that DES circulars may be well-meaning, but they aren't exactly the precursers of shattering change. Just try getting your local school to open during the summer holidays.

But we can give some examples of good practice. Cyril Poster, presently head of Sheppey School, has described his experience as Head of Lawrence Weston School, in Bristol.[85] There a public library was located *in* the school. That seems an excellent way to 'open' the school, which is the first step towards opening its facilities to outsiders, which is the first step towards giving the community an active function in the school. At Lawrence Weston School parents came to learn in the language labs (!) and domestic-science rooms. Saturday morning film shows were held in the school, and a pigeon-fanciers-club operated. The scheme was fine, but we must reiterate; the breakthrough in education will come when the community comes into schools to help, not just to use an empty room for a committee meeting or to hold adult education classes. But Lawrence Weston School at least dropped some of the institutional barriers.

In Leicestershire the community colleges have also set out along this path, using school buildings not just for the education of young people, but also for classes for adults from the local community, and for recreation purposes. There are now twelve community colleges in Leicestershire, the first being opened at Ashby-de-la-Zouch in 1954.

Thirty years before that, Henry Morris, Chief Education Officer for Cambridgeshire, was looking closely at the education of children in rural areas. He saw that many of them, on leaving the village primary school, were travelling to get their secondary education in urban areas. In consequence they were divorced from their rural roots and culture, rather like Joe and Isaac. On the other hand, he recognized the economic considerations behind these peripatetic arrangements. But Henry Morris proposed that 'village colleges' be set up, with part of their function being to provide secondary education for children from the surrounding area. So a college would be set up in one village, and would receive pupils from surrounding tributary villages. In the village colleges the curriculum would have 'a strong rural bias'. But 'education' was to be only a part of the village college's function, for it was also to be a focus of community life, in the fullest sense. Primary, secondary, further and adult education would all be based there, so that, in the village college

> ... there would be no 'leaving school' – the child would enter at three and leave the college only in extreme old age.[86]

Morris wasn't proposing that the school-leaving age be raised to ninety-four. He saw, rather, that you should have education 'on tap' when you needed it. This idea reminds us of the 'voucher system' of education, which Everett Reimer and other writers have proposed. They suggest that people 'spend' their vouchers for education on what they like, when they choose to learn. So the urge to learn book keeping at ninety-four might find you back in school in a class of very mixed ages.

But there is more to it than that. The village college would cater for the needs of the community with social and recreational facilities, and be a community centre *par excellence*. The local clinic, library, careers office, nursery, infant welfare clinic, would all be located there. There would be rooms for all local organizations to meet. There would be billiard rooms, even. To clarify the idea, here is a description, from R. J. McCloy, the Assistant Education Officer for Cambridgeshire, of a village college which he was showing to visitors: 'At one end of the building a rabbit show was being held, and at the other a wedding reception ...' Or, in Henry Morris's words:

> We must institutionalize our places of education so that they become centres of corporate life, and not congeries of class-room for discourse and instruction.[87]

We did raise our eye-brows at 'institutionalize', but the statement as a whole deserves attention, for it applies to every community.

Many approve of village colleges because they make economic sense, showing how an educational establishment can utilize resources, year in, year out, day and night. But Morris was really concerned with *social* issues, we believe. The first was the loss of secondary-age children to urban areas, and their consequent irrelevant, non-rural education. Also he recognized that the village college could keep rural communities alive and flourishing. They could keep people together through

> .. a grouping and coordination of all the educational and social agencies, whether statutory or voluntary, which now exist in isolation in the countryside; an amalgamation which, while preserving the individuality and function of each, will assemble them into a whole, and make possible their expression for the first time in a new institution, single but many-sided, for the countryside.[88]

'Institution' worried us again, but read on:

> The whole welfare of communities, and the vigour and prosperity of their social life in particular, depend on the extent to which centres of unfettered initiative can be developed within them – that is, on freedom. The object of the village college, therefore, will be to enhance, and not diminish, the freedom and initiative of the voluntary association of the countryside.[89]

In other words, if your 'institution' is big enough to embrace everybody, the 'exclusivity', that root of institutional evil, will cease to prevent participation. Your community becomes your institution.

The first village college was opened at Sawston in 1930, and since then a dozen have been established. But Morris' thinking had influence beyond his own education authority. Besides Lawrence Weston School (Cyril Poster worked in a village college before going there), other 'community schools' appeared here and there. Wyndham School, in Cumberland, is an example.

The Plowden Report *Children and their Primary Schools*[90] led, amongst other things, to the designation of 'Educational Priority Areas' (EPAs), a token of positive discrimination in favour of deprived urban areas. One plank of the EPA platform was the idea of the primary school as a community school.

> The community school – the process and organization of learning through all social relations – must be seen as essential to educational advance in EPAs. Permanent Community Education Task Forces should be created to establish these locally appropriate linkages of school and community....[91]

Eric Midwinter, who directed the 1968–71 Liverpool EPA project, puts it more practically and clearly:

> Herein lies the full meaning of the community school which, according to Plowden, should initially be established in deprived areas. It is not merely a school that welcomes in the parents or is open in the evening for father to do a bit of fretwork. It is a thorough-going device to identify school and community in every aspect of the life of each for the better health of both. In a world in which, it is often said, the individual is lost against the grey, anonymous and faceless backcloth of society, there is possibly here a hope for the regeneration and rejuvenation of wholesome and dynamic community life.[92]

While the E P As provide a gratifying opportunity to experiment with 'alternatives within' the system, the free schools, to which we referred earlier, were not just providing alternative content. Their structure of small units, with education focused on the child's needs and interests and on the character of the local community, are a great contrast to the two thousand-strong units which are beginning to form the pattern of state education. The latter are a response to the needs of economy and efficiency alone.

So the crucial issue is one of function. For in the community school the community must have a function, an active one, enabling human talent of all kinds to be fully exercised. Conversely, the school itself must have a function. It will be more than a meeting place, a vibrant centre of community life – though that it should be. It will have a function in the community, learning in it and servicing its needs. To this we must add that the school environment will be small, community-oriented. It will preferably not be purpose-built, except in rural areas where buildings are not already available. Taking a lesson from free schools, old houses, shops or factories could be used. It is important that teachers come from the local community. This is inherent in all we have said. In the Victorian village school the teacher was well-known, because he was part of the community and one of its features. Now he is just another professional. A strange separate figure.

All well and good if the school can be, on top of this, a nodal point – a community centre. There is nothing worse than imposing community centres willy nilly, even the new type of school/community centre we propose. The community has centres already. They are called pubs and clubs. So let us add them to Henry Morris's list of educational and social agencies. Morris was dead right in pointing the community to the focal point of the college. We might imagine, therefore, if we accept that what he was saying about rural communities is applicable to our urban and suburban deserts, that every conceivable statutory, voluntary and community function is based in the school. A gargantuan fifty-acre complex of social workers, probation officers, youth clubs, police stations, cinemas, meeting rooms, assembly halls, maternity clinics, with a hundred children and a few teachers submerged beneath it all? No, for if the school is a nodal point for the community, in our picture, then the statutory provisions will become, in time, small appendages to community initiatives and involvement. We described this process earlier. The community will very largely look after itself. Smaller schools will be the springboard for its activities. As we have said, the pub is probably the most common centre of community life at present. It may well be that we should base our schools there.

'Teacher' will always be needed, to enable and direct children to the learning that they need to fulfil their potential. 'Teacher' will cease to be a professional purveyor of knowledge and become an enabler, and a bit of all the other professionals in one person. Henry Morris said that the role of the village college warden was one of, 'I stand amongst you as he that serveth'.[93] That, surely, should apply to every teacher, and every school.

Class structure in the community school mixes young and old freely. Adults will be found among classes of teenagers more and more as 'leisure' (or unemployment) increases. In earlier chapters we stressed that schools in their present forms would be limited in undertaking community projects. For schools in their present forms are for young people. When schools are for all people, young and old, handicapped and able-bodied, they will be more effective in servicing the community, for every age, every skill, every ability will be found there.

The community school will not close and open its doors for 'terms' or 'school days'. It will be open all the time. People will come and go without awe, fear or hindrance. To the rabbit show and the wedding reception will be added groups of people meeting, groups of people learning together, groups of people servicing one another's needs: interacting, if you like.

Well, that's it. We didn't set out to be doctrinaire, to provide a blueprint for community action, community schooling and de-schooling. There isn't one, and therein lies the virtue of community action, community schooling and de-schooling. Communities will work out their own prototypes. We merely offer optimism, and the conviction that it can be done. For we are not alone in finding today's schools and today's communities lacking. All human beings have a right to interact with their fellows, yet they are becoming isolated from them. All human beings have a right to an education relevant to their needs in a situation which enables them to interact with their fellows. All human beings have a right to a little education, for a change.

Notes

1. T. E. B. Howarth, High Master, St Paul's School, Inaugural Conference, Council for Preservation of Educational Standards, 1972.

2. *Half Our Future*, HMSO, 1963.

3. ibid.

4. ibid.

5. ibid.

6. ibid.

7. CSV poster, 1972.

8. *Task Force*, by Tim Dartington, Mitchell-Beazley Ltd and Task Force, 1971.

9. Schools Council Working Paper no. 17, *Community Service and the Curriculum*, HMSO, 1968.

10. ibid.

11. ibid.

12. ibid.

13. In Leicestershire's community colleges the words 'Community Education' have a different meaning. They mean education of the community through adult education classes in schools, etc.

14. Extract from DES/Welsh Office circular on *Raising the School-Leaving Age*, sent to all schools (Circular no. 8/71 (139/71 in Wales).

15. Aves Committee Report, *The Voluntary Worker in the Social Services*, HMSO, 1969.

16. Seebohm Report, HMSO, 1970.

17. It means 'Cot and Chair'!

18. *The Times Educational Supplement*, 7 January 1972.

19. *Teaching Adult Illiterates*, by Cliff Edwards, CSV Project 71, 1971.

20. ibid.

21. ibid.

22. ibid.

23. ibid.

24. *Glasgow Hospitals' Scheme for Schools*, by Margaret Roddan, CSV Project 71, 1971.

25. ibid.

26. ibid.

27. ibid.

28. ibid.

29. ibid.

30. ibid.

31. ibid.

32. ibid.

33. *The Use of Origami in Community Service*, by Paul Castles, CSV Sack, 1972.

34. *Daily Telegraph.*

35. Ivan Illich, in *Deschooling Society* (Penguin 1973), and Everett Reimer, in *School is Dead* (Penguin, 1971), discuss in far more detail how this failure is occurring.

36. *Access for the Disabled*, by Linda Thomas, CSV Project 71, 1970.

37. *Sunday Times.*

38. *Guardian.*

39. Reproduced from the bulletin of the Ramblers Association, *Footpath Worker*, 1971.

40. *Gypsies and Other Travellers*, HMSO, 1967.

41. *Sevenoaks Chronicle*, 2 June 1972.

42. *Involvement with Children*, by J. R. Hooper, CSV Project 71, 1971.

43. ibid.

44. ibid.

45. *A Mural for a Playgroup*, by Keith Tomkinson, CSV Sack, 1972.

46. ibid.

47. ibid.

48. *Half Way There*, by Alwyn Thomas, Schools Council Design and Craft Project bulletin, 'Survey', 1970.

49. ibid.

50. *Projects for Real*, by W. P. C. Mills, CSV Project 71, 1971.

51. ibid.

52. ibid.

53. *Community Service as Part of the ESN School Curriculum*, by George Maxted, CSV Project 71, 1971.

54. ibid.

55. *Rubbish*, by Hawley, Gurr, Williams, Walton and Walker, CSV Project 71, 1971.

56. *Education for Self Reliance*, by Julius Nyerere, President of the United Republic of Tanzania, Association for International Development, Paterson, New Jersey.

57. *Sevenoaks Chronicle.*

58. *Youth Tutors Youth*, by H. Anderson and J. Green, CSV, 1970.

59. ibid.

60. A local newspaper account described in 'Tutoring by students', by Professor H. A. Thelen, in *School Review*, vol. 77, no. 3, September 1969, University of Chicago Department of Education.

61. *Guardian*, 'Little Red Schoolkids', 26 May 1972.

62. From 'Tutoring by students', by Professor H. A. Thelen; see note 60.

63. 'Underacheivers in the Junior High', in *Impact*, the School District of University City, Missouri.

64. *The Haverstock Tutoring Scheme*, by L. K. Myers and J. Rolfe, CSV Sack, 1971.

65. ibid.

66. All from 'Every child a teacher', by Gartner, Kohler, Reissman, in *Childhood Education*, October 1971 (USA).

67. *Education for Self Reliance*, Julius Nyerere, see note 56.

68. ibid.

69. ibid.

70. ibid.

71. ibid.

72. 'Eleanor Rigby', Beatles song.

73. 'He ain't heavy, he's my brother', Russel and Scott.

74. 'Take a load off granny', song from *Easy Rider*.

75. 'Our world', Blue Mink song.

76. 'A little bit of love', song by Free.

77. *Enclosures Then and Now*, by Pat Kendell, CSV Sack 1971.

78. *Music and Community Service*, by Michael Walker, CSV Sack, 1972.

79. *Sunday Times*, 16 July 1972.

80. 'Sparking off interest – David Wright did it with postmarks', *Bulletin of Environmental Education*, no. 15, July 1972.

81. *Pedestrians are People*, by Keith Wheeler, CSV Sack, 1972.

82. *Education for Self Reliance*, Julius Nyerere, see note 56.

83. ibid.

84. ibid.

85. See Cyril Poster's chapter in *Headship in the* 1970s, edited by Bryan Allen, Blackwell 1969.

86. *The Village College*, by Henry Morris, Cambridge University Press, 1924.

87. ibid.

88. ibid.

89. ibid.

90. A report of the Central Advisory Council for Education, 1967.

91. The 'Halsey Programme' quoted in *Priority News*, May 1972. A. H. Halsey was National Director of the 1968–71 EPA Projects.

92. *Projections – an Educational Priority Area at Work'*, Ward Lock Educational, 1972.

93. *The Village College*, by Henry Morris, see note 86.

Education For Democracy

Edited by David Rubenstein and Colin Stoneman

The time for a radical manifesto on British education is long overdue. For over twenty-five years the struggle to democratize our system has been held back by those who see the proper function of education as the production of an élite and, as the most efficient means of effecting this, the labelling of children as A's or D's at the earliest possible opportunity. Those children who do not meet the requirements of the current élite have had some reason to be disconsolate about their fate.

Here at last – appropriately at a time when the 'backlash' is receiving all the attention, if not actually gaining the upper hand – is a bold definition of the nature and purpose of 'education for democracy'.

The contributors to this collection, all of whom have to grapple daily with these problems on the lecture-hall or classroom floor, do not attempt to put forward a single, easy solution. But whether they are writing about the content of the primary curriculum or university examinations, about slum schools or the new technology of learning, there is one fundamental belief which they all hold in common. They demand an education system which cares about *all* children, regardless of race, class or intelligence, and which helps to build a democratic society by upholding the qualities of compassion and respect within its own walls.

'This is a thought provoking and stimulating book which raises the question as to what education for democracy should be'
Tribune

Compulsory Miseducation

Paul Goodman

Much of the sharpest and most fundamental thinking about education has been coming from America. This book is one of five titles published simultaneously by Penguin Education. It would be wrong to call these writers a school – they are widely different in stance and style. But they are united, firstly by their readiness to think of education in (literally) radical ways and to propose radical solutions; secondly, by their deep concern that education should exist primarily for the benefit of those who learn; and lastly, and above all, by their conviction that education – in the modern world as in America – has reached crisis point.

'When, at a meeting, I offer that perhaps we already have too much formal schooling and that, under present conditions, the more we get the less education we will get, the others look at me oddly and proceed to discuss how to get more money for schools and how to upgrade the schools. I realize suddenly that I am confronting a mass superstition.'

The mass superstition in question, which is the target of this classic and inconoclastic work, is that education can only be achieved by the use of institutions like the school. Paul Goodman argues that, on the contrary, subjecting young people to institutionalized learning stunts and distorts their natural intellectual development, makes them hostile to the very idea of education, and finally turns out regimented, competitive citizens likely only to aggravate our current social ills. He prescribes an increased involvement in the natural learning patterns of family and community, and of the sort of relationships fostered in master–apprentice situations.

'Its radical questioning of the whole system is a revelation to people who have been schooled to take the system for granted' Ian Lister *The Times Higher Education Supplement*

Deschooling Society

Ivan D. Illich

Is schooling the same thing as education? Obviously not. We all learn day by day, and most of us, to be honest, can find little in our lives which schooling has directly and profoundly influenced. Two questions emerge. What is it then that has given schooling such enormous and widespread prestige in all societies throughout the world? And what is it that schooling actually does if its educational function is in doubt?

Ivan Illich argues in this eloquent and persuasive book that school has the prestige it does because it is one of the major means by which the status quo is preserved. It is not only inefficient in terms of education, but also profoundly divisive. *Deschooling Society* has already become a classic statement of a new and disturbing view of the school as an institution. It is amply possible to disagree with Illich: it is hardly possible to ignore him.

'His assault on the school . . . demands to be considered seriously' Peter Jenkins, *Guardian.*

Deschooling Society is one of the most genuine subversive books in that it amounts to a radical reinterpretation of social reality' David Gow *Scotsman.*

'Illich and Reimer have asked some of the profoundest questions about education today' Ian Lister *The Times Educational Supplement.*

School is Dead

Everett Reimer

Most of the children in the world are not in school. Most of those who are drop out as soon as possible. Most countries in the world can only afford to give their children the barest minimum of education, while the costs of schooling are everywhere rising faster than enrolments, and faster than national income. Schools are for most people what the author calls 'institutional props for privilege', and yet at the same time they are the major instruments of social mobility. But at what cost in terms of true learning, true creativity, true democracy? And at what ultimate cost to the societies which perpetuate themselves in this way?

This is the background to Everett Reimer's important, wide-ranging and intelligent book. The most urgent priority, he argues, is for a consideration of *alternatives* in education – alternative content, organization and finance. Above all, we urgently need alternative views of education itself, its nature and possible functions in the society of the future.

'Illich and Reimer have asked some of the profoundest questions about education today'.
Ian Lister *The Times Higher Education Supplement*.

'The case against universal compulsory schooling is a substantial one and Everett Reimer thumps it out in chapter after chapter'
Christopher Price *New Statesman*.

Children in Distress

Alec Clegg and Barbara Megson

Two out of every hundred children have to be given direct help by the State – whether it be psychiatric, social or medical.

But are these the only children 'in distress'? What about those children who do not qualify for State help?

Alec Clegg and Barbara Megson estimate that perhaps 12 per cent of our children desperately need help, but do not qualify to receive it. *Children in Distress* paints an agonizing picture of child distress, based on the authors' long experience in educational administration. They argue that it is the schools – in daily contact with the children – that are the agencies best suited to help this large and saddening section of our child population.

'... this book, containing a wealth of information and ideas based on the experience of very many schools, can help teachers who want to help their problem pupils, but just do not know how to start. It can help them, probably more than any other single volume' *The Times Educational Supplement*.

Spare the Child

W. David Wills

Approved schools were originally set up for the children of the 'perishing and dangerous classes'; nowadays they contain 'children in trouble'. Yet if the labels have changed, many of the schools have not: too often the young offender is treated as morally and socially inferior, and subjected to a harsh regime of character training. *Spare the Child* is a remarkable account of how the staff of an orthodox approved school is trying, with vision and tenacity, to convert it into a therapeutic community. Their concern was to rid the school of its hierarchial and repressive structure, and to establish instead a community which could provide the care and understanding of which the boys had previously been deprived. What was encountered was violent hostility to such changes from some of the staff, and, even more alarmingly, the existence among the boys of an established and vicious subculture which mirrored all too accurately the official system of rewards and punishments. As the author shows in his eloquent and sympathetic narrative, some of the problems which arose as the changeover took place were peculiar to the Cotswold Community, others were inherent in the task of overthrowing traditional approaches and attitudes in the child-care service. This book demonstrates vividly how modern therapeutic methods can transform those institutions to which society entrusts the care of its problem children.

Cultural Action for Freedom

Paulo Freire

Paulo Freire's *Cultural Action for Freedom* is the educational process itself, and, particularly and crucially, teaching literacy to adults. Within his definition of that process learners sssume from the beginning the role of creative subjects. Learning is not a matter of memorizing and repeating given words, syllables and phrases, but rather of reflecting critically on the process of reading and writing itself and on the profound significance of language. As the most important vehicle of cultural transmission language, and therefore literacy, must be used, developed and given meaning by those whose will it must express.

In seeking to challenge the conceptual and cultural domination that prevailed in the slums and villages of Latin America, Freire developed a highly original and spectacularly successful method of teaching literacy. In this book he outlines the principles which underlay that method and their implications.

Pedagogy of the Oppressed

Paulo Freire

In Paulo Freire's hands literacy is a weapon for social change. Education once again becomes the means by which men can perceive, interpret, criticize and finally transform the world about them.

Freire's attack on the 'culture of silence' inhabited by the vast numbers of illiterate peasants in Brazil's poorest areas has contributed in an extraordinary way to the development of a sense of purpose and identity among the oppressed and demoralized majority. His work is the result of a process of reflection in the midst of a struggle to create a new social order. His is the authentic voice of the Third World, but his methodology and philosophy are also important in the industrialized countries where a new culture of silence threatens to dominate an overconsuming and overmanaged population, where education too often means merely socialization. In contrast, Freire's approach concentrates upon the ability to deal creatively with reality.

State School

R. F. Mackenzie

When he became headmaster of a secondary modern school in the Scottish coalfields, R. F. Mackenzie found himself in charge of children whose lives promised to become as derelict as their surroundings – unhappy, delinquent, their futures blocked by a joyless and, to them, impossible tradition of academic education.

This anthology of extracts from his writings describes his fight to provide them with an education which was both imaginative and relevant. Trips in the Scottish countryside, which were the children's first experience of independence and of the beauty of the land they lived in, convinced him that the school should acquire a permanent base in the Highlands, an ambition which thrust him into a long and bitter struggle with an officialdom which prized narrow restrictions more than such dreams. There were other dreams, too, and other defeats: staff who betrayed his ideal of a school free from authoritarian modes of discipline, delinquent children who tried, unsuccessfully, to keep out of trouble. But these pages speak of anything but defeat: they describe the authentic feel of the experience which education should provide, especially for the underprivileged, and demonstrate convincingly how good the victory will be when it is, finally, won.

R. F. Mackenzie is now headmaster of Summerhill Comprehensive School in Aberdeen.

Death at an Early Age

Jonathan Kozol

The descruction of the hearts and minds of Negro children in the Boston public schools.

The discrimination hst has made second-class citizens of one generation of coloured adults will as surely disinherit their children, future British citizens now in our classrooms, unless we urgently root out from ourselves – parents, neighbours, teachers, administrators – and from our teaching, our school books, our assumptions about language and thinking the subtle prejudices that, with a multitude of small cuts, wound the heart and mind. *Death at an Early Age* is a moving personal testament from America: it also carries an urgent message for our society. Time for action may be passing faster than we think.

The Multi-Racial School

Edited by Julia McNeal and Margaret Rogers

Our schools have a crucial role to play in responding to the challenges of a multi-racial society. *The Multi-Racial School* shows how a number of teachers, unprepared by their training and ill equipped with materials, each devised a strategy to cope with the situation in their own urban primary or secondary school. Whether their solution was to set up a language unit or centre within the school, or to tackle the problem of inter-racial hostility in the local community by improving home–school relationships, or to move towards mixed-ability groups in response to the diverse realities of a multi-racial class, one fact became generally apparent: they were dealing not with an 'immigrant problem', but with a group of children whose presence served to uncover and highlight existing deficiencies in the schools.

Nothing less than a redefinition of the educational needs of their children was being demanded of these teachers. Their essays demonstrate what can be done, through practical experiement and by positive determination, to make the educational system responsible to the multi-racial character of schools today.

Letter to a Teacher
School of Barbiana

Afterword by Lord Boyle of Handsworth

Eight young Italian boys from the mountains outside Florence wrote this passionate and eloquent book. It took them a year. Simply and clearly, with some devastating statistical analysis of the Italian education system, they set out to show the ways in which attitudes towards class, behaviour, language and subject-matter militate against the poor. They describe, too, the reforms they propose, and the methods they use in their own school – the School of Barbiana, started under the guidance of a parish priest and now run entirely by the children.

This remarkable book was written for the parents of the Italian poor. But it is about the poor everywhere: their anger is the anger of every worker and peasant who sees middle-class children absorbed effortlessly into the schools as teacher's favourites.

Letter to a Teacher was a best-seller in Italy and has been published subsequently in many languages. The School of Barbiana was awarded the prize of the Italian Physical Society, usually reserved for promising physicists, for the statistical achievement involved in the book.

'... this marvel of a book ... a masterpiece of protest ... an original work of Literature ... I have read no book on education that has left me so uncomfortably aware of the injustice done daily in our schools to great masses of our fellow human beings' *Edward Blishen*